EXTRA INNINGS
My Life in Baseball

REGNERY GATEWAY
• Chicago •

MINOSO

EXTRA INNINGS

My Life in Baseball

with

Fernando Fernandez

and

Robert Kleinfelder

Published by Regnery Gateway, Inc., 360 West Superior Street, Chicago, Illinois 60610-0890.

Manufactured in the United States of America.
ISBN: 0-89526-625-3

Library of Congress Catalog Card Number: 82-42903

With deepest appreciation and humble gratitude I dedicate this book to all who influenced my career, particularly baseball fans everywhere, and especially those who fill Chicago's Comiskey Park.

I want to extend my deep appreciation to all who contributed to the appearance of this book. First and foremost to Fernando J. Fernandez who initially distilled hours of conversation and thousands of files into readable material; and to Robert A. Kleinfelder for his Herculean effort in the final touches.

To Maria Carlo, Audrey Braesel, Dennis Christiansen, Duane Hayden, Linda Barrett, Janice Martin, Olga Santos, Norma Barrett, and Cheryl Peterson, my sincere thanks for the research, verification, and typing help they provided.

Special thanks to Public Relations Director William J. Guilfoile and Historian Clifford S. Kachline of the Baseball Hall of Fame without whose tireless contribution this book would have been much less.

For the photo contributions of Tony Inzerillo; the counsel of Mark Muscarello; the encouragement and help of Monte Irvin in the Office of the Commissioner; and last but not least, to the Chicago White Sox organization, particularly Pauline Allyn; and Jerry Campagna of C & K Distributors without whom this book would not have been published; *I am eternally grateful.*

In Minnie Minoso's 35 years as an active professional player (1945-1980) in Cuba, the U.S., and Mexico his incomplete statistics (none are available for his Negro League days) of 2,608 games, 16,043 times at bat, 2,801 hits, and .290 lifetime batting average indicate he probably played in more professional baseball games than anyone else in the history of the sport.

Top of the 1st

My feelings that day were hard to describe: impossible, in fact. As a kid in Cuba, I had grown up with baseball in my blood. My heroes were ball players and every spare minute I had—and some even that I couldn't spare—were spent on the baseball diamond. During those hot and sunny days I gave everything I had, every ounce of energy, to be like my idols.

And here I was, 27 years old, but at heart still that kid on the sandlots of Cuba, starting in the outfield of the Cleveland Indians. The year was 1949, and the Indians "brought me north" from their spring training camp in Tucson, Arizona, where I had batted .400. For a contract boasting the grand sum of $1,000 a month I became a proud member of one of the best teams in major league baseball.

My debut was a moment I'll never forget. I was playing right field in place of Bob Kennedy. The great Larry Doby was in center and Dale Mitchell, who possessed one of the league's top batting averages, was in left.

It was a special occasion in another way, for I joined a team having two other pioneer black players in major league baseball—Doby, the first black in the American League, and the immortal Satchel Paige. The Indians that year fielded such superstars as playing manager Lou Boudreau, Joe Gordon, Bob Lemon, Mike Garcia and probably the best pitcher in baseball, Bob Feller.

It was a dream come true. And, in those spring days of '49, midst the cheering of the record crowds at Cleveland's giant Municipal Stadium, my thoughts often drifted back to the land of my birth, to the people I loved. I was so very proud and honored to represent Cuba, baseball-loving Cuba, in the major leagues.

How far away it all seemed...

El Perico, a town of 3,000 people, set in the rich sugar cane land that was the foundation of the Cuban economy. Here, during the "Roaring Twenties," or as it was called in Cuba, the Dance of the Millions, I was born. The island's economy prospered and my proud parents predicted a great future for their son. But Cuba, like the rest of the world, suffered the nightmare of the Great Depression, and in 1929 my family was forced to give up our comfortable home in El Perico. We took refuge in what could only be described as a shanty in the sugar cane area of La Lonja.

Although our one-crop economy had its drawbacks, I, and I know many other Cuban ballplayers, credit our native sugar cane for much of our success in sports. The sugar cane was always accessible to me and when combined with our meager rations, gave me strength and stamina. Often I have been asked to share my secret of perenniel health and my longevity in baseball. I must point to the Cuban sugar cane (the richest yield in the world) as being instrumental in building my strength and physical stamina.

My childhood surroundings may have been humble, but they were healthy; so simple, peaceful and consoling, where everything breathed life, humanity and vigor.

My mother, Cecilia Armas, was a widow when she married Carlos Arrieta Lopez. My father, a strong, robust man, also raised my four half-brothers and sisters, Cirilo, Francisco, Juanita and Flora Minoso. Why was I called Minoso instead of my real name, Arrieta? Those who saw me from childhood playing ball with my half-brothers Minoso began calling me Minoso, too. In Cuba, people don't make distinctions between first and last names in addressing others, whether adults or children. "Hey, Minoso; Listen, Minoso," they would call, and I really didn't mind. Later when I went to play baseball in Havana, a hundred miles away, I thought, "Well, here I am in my country's capital. Everybody already knows me as Minoso. If I change my name back to Arrieta there could be confusion and I could lose what popularity I already enjoy." Thus, I am known as Minoso. When I became an American citizen, I legally changed my name to Orestes Minoso. Nonetheless, in my personal diary I maintain my complete baptismal name, Saturnino Orestes Arrieta Armas.

Which brings me to a point I believe best clarified as soon as possible. Where did I get the nickname, "Minnie." Well, Lou Boudreau claims he coined it when he managed me during my brief stint with the Indians. I'm not entirely convinced. I can't really remember who really "baptized" me with "Minnie," or why. Perhaps because I'm only 5'11" or it's short for Minoso. I recall the time in my rookie year with the Sox, that I went to see a dentist at his offices at 63rd and Cottage Grove. Dr. Robinson called out "Minnie" during my visit and I thought he was addressing me. Instead, he was calling to his assistant, a young girl. Which caused me to inquire if the name "Minnie" is masculine or feminine. Much to my relief, he said it could be used either way. In any event, Chicago identified me with that name and I became comfortable with it. I even made it part of my legal name in the United States.

I attended public schools in El Perico, but, admittedly, didn't excell in scholarship. My love was sports. My one dream was to become a professional baseball player, a hero. I determined to be one at all costs, over the strong objections of my poor mother. As mothers are prone to do, she always imagined the dangers and misfortunes of sports. Though her outlook may have seemed somewhat pessimistic, in my case she wasn't far off target. Her Orestes went on to establish a record in the majors of being hit 189 times by pitched balls. I also sustained a near-fatal skull fracture in an unforgettable collision with the left field fence in St. Louis.

My parents did not have the financial resources to send me to college or the polytechnic institute. I was an experienced farmer, able to plow the land, plant, fertilize, weed and cut the sugar cane. But I was a farmboy who'd sooner have a bat in his hand than a farm implement.

My first team was made up of farm boys, nine and ten years of age. An organized system of youth baseball was lacking in my country and our first team in La Lonja had no funds for uniforms, spiked shoes or other necessary equipment. We were, indeed, a strange looking team, with our uniforms made of old flour sacks. For equipment our older brothers managed to get us cracked bats and shabby gloves which we had to repair before we could play.

Actually this lack of first-rate equipment (sometimes we were even forced to play bare-handed), shaped the talents of many Cuban and other Hispanic-American baseball players. We were forced to use our raw talents more, a necessity which helped many Hispanics break into organized clubs in Cuba, Mexico, the Caribbean and, the ultimate goal, the big leagues in the United States. My boyhood idol was Martin Dihigo, recently elected to baseball's Hall of Fame, because he had the same humble beginnings as me, and was nonetheless able to become a superstar.

Our favorite playing field was a grazing field near the sugar mill. The foreman was less than enthusiastic because we tended to tear up the hedges and let the cattle escape. Still, all Cubans loved sports, including sugar mill owners, and we were allowed to play—one of the conditions being that Orestes Minoso would be responsible for guarding the hedges. We also agreed not to eat the sugar cane, though we would have welcomed the energy it brought, much as athletes in the United States appreciate candy bars.

Most of the 160 sugar mills in Cuba had baseball teams, comprised of employees and very often paid players. Our Espana Mill always had a good team, often fielding retired professional players. These mill and factory teams sometimes played teams from the Cuban Amateur League, which boasted such stars as major league ace Sandy Consuegra. These were the players—amateurs and semi-pros—who I watched, admired and from whom I learned how the great game of baseball should be played.

Watching these great players and playing on my own La Lonja team made me more determined than ever to be a professional ball player. When I was twelve years old, in addition to playing center field, third base and pitching, I was the team's manager. At twelve years of age! We played two or three times a week and with each passing week I grew more ambitious. I wanted to be tops every time I slid into a base, every time I made a diving catch of a line drive, every time I hit a home run. I wanted to be the best! I realize I wasn't alone. All young Cuban ballplayers had the same dream; first the Cuban League of professional baseball and then the big leagues of the U.S., the most coveted of all goals, whether the young athlete is from La Lonja, Havana, Alabama or Pennsylvania. And we Cubans knew it could be done, because great Cuban stars had already made it in the majors: Alejandro Olms, Armando Marsans, Adolph Luque.

I credit my success in the sport I love to a great many Cuban athletes whom I copied in my early life. However, there is one skill which I wasn't really taught; it was a skill which came to me naturally. That skill was running, and running barefoot, because I had but one pair of shoes which I saved for special occasions. It was not unusual for small boys to run barefoot at great speeds. Running, running, running...a habit that I found entertaining and exhilarating—always running. I used to practice playing center field with a friend who would hit the ball over my head in order for me to perfect back-peddling. He would see to it that I caught fly balls and charged liners—all on the run. In so doing, each day I gained speed and dexterity. It was habit-forming, this running. Later, Chicago White Sox Manager Paul Richards, after watching me run the bases, named me the "Cuban Comet." I credit this early running with eventually making it "second nature" for me to transform easy grounders into hits, extend singles into doubles and steal bases almost at will.

I always felt that the difference between victory and defeat was giving more than 100 percent during a game. Often, whether you got on base or not was determined, not so much by the strength of your hit, but by how fast you ran. Such running also makes the game more colorful, more competitive and creates suspense whenever you try to reach a base. Let's face it, I made the pitchers nervous and I always believed that winning teams had players who were base-stealing threats. This is the way I feel about the game I love, because it also makes baseball fun, and to me, baseball has always been fun.

As a sixteen-year-old, I was determined to forsake pitching in favor of the outfield. Why? Because if I hurt my pitching arm, I'd be through, but an every-day position player wouldn't have that worry. Before I "retired" my pitching arm, I had one last memorable day. A team of young bloods from El Reglita had beaten my beloved La Lonja team badly, and boasted about it afterwards. We had to redeem ourselves, and I was in charge of putting together a team for a return game. The date was set and I decided to pitch my last game. What a farewell it was: a no-hitter, with sixteen strikeouts! We were redeemed!

Bottom of the 1st

How hard were things in Depression-era Cuba? Though I recall having to sleep in hammocks, the lack of running water and buying on credit during "dead time" for the farming crews, one incident stands out in my mind: Minoso vs. the cow.

I was about to start in a ball game, but was wearing my "Sunday Shirt," a Hawaiian print. I was the only one I owned. To keep it from getting sweaty from playing, I hung it on a wire fence. As luck would have it, a cow soon came by, snatched my prized shirt and ran off with it. The Hawaiian delicacy must have been to her liking because she began eating it. My teammates and I chased the beast, but even well-conditioned young Cubans had trouble corraling a cow. So, with a rock and a pitch that would have made Bob Feller envious, I nailed the beast in the leg. It never walked the same. No one else ever knew that it owed its limp to Minoso, because my friends said nothing. And my precious shirt? There was little left but the buttons.

There were other cows in my life, though. I was somewhat of a *vaquero,* or cowboy, There were cattle in our pasture and, astride my chubby little filly, my chores included rounding up the calves every morning, at 4AM and separating them from the cows, so the cows could be milked. I was a dashing sight (not in the least, of course, to impress the girls), sporting my boots and Texas sombrero and gloves. I always wore a machete in my belt and liberally used the lasso. As a vaquero, I also learned to tame oxen, handle wagons, break in the animals and teach the colts to jump. The girls admired that teenage dashing Minoso.

It was while working on the farm that I nearly saw my baseball career come to a close. I was on tractor and my father pulled up the oxen wagon to turn the posts. Somehow my leg got caught on the wagon and the flesh tore off. My father rushed me on an electric railway handcar to a doctor who, unfortunately, was drunk from a weekend of celebration. He did what he could, bandaging my leg, but warning us that because the wound was so deep, healing would be difficult. How right he was! When time came to take off the bandage, it was found it had adhered to the bone. There was the danger of infection and possible amputation. Luckily, the bandage was removed and my wound eventually healed, thanks to my youth and to Providence.

Not long after, I accidentally stabbed myself with the machete in the same leg, same spot. So I spent fifteen more days in a rest cure, listening to my father complaining that if I wanted to be a ball player, I'd have to take better care of myself.

My poor father had further cause for remorse later when I fell from a mango tree, losing consciousness for five minutes. Another time I got caught between two horses, one of which decided to start kicking. Result, two cracked ribs and almost a punctured lung. Then there was my hernia, the time I was gored in the arm by a bull, the day a motorbus sideswiped my wrist. . . . But enough. Is it any wonder that I set so many records at being hurt when I was in the major leagues?

I became a teamster with an oxen wagon in 1942, shortly after my mother died. It was an important job, almost like being a baseball manager in the United States. Young as I was, I had the best team of oxen in the region, the pay was good and it was a secure job. But baseball still flowed in my veins and on the days I wasn't working, I was on the ballfield. I organized a quality team, superior to any others in the region, and those who watched me play used to say, "That boy is going to be a great player!"

For two years I worked the cane harvest with my team of oxen. But then I made one of the greatest decisions of my life; I went to Havana to play ball. This venture to the capital happened in a way which I'll never forget.

One day, I was clearing weeds from a corn patch on the farm of Juan Llins. An idea occurred to me and I went to the Espana Company to see a boy named Humberto Fernandez, another baseball player and driver.

"Hey, Humberto," I called. "We're going to write a letter as if it were coming from Havana. It will be in your handwriting, saying that they're expecting me to play ball. I'll dictate it and make it sound urgent, saying I'm the only one who can fill the position. Mail it from El Perico. When it arrives here, come and give it to me while I'm clearing ground with the guys."

As planned, the next day, about 11AM, as we were shoveling under the hot sun, Humberto arrived and called, "Hey, Orestes, I've got a letter for you." I acted surprised, began to read it, and said (with an air of disinterest) that I couldn't possibly go to Havana. Juan Llins exclaimed, "Hey, what do they want you to do?" I gave him the letter and he immediately shouted, "Get your clothes together and go to Havana."

I must admit, I put on a good show. I argued, but Juan insisted I should go, that this was my future, that I should not turn my back on destiny. Trying to keep a straight face, I said I had to finish my shoveling. Juan said no, I must immediately prepare to move to the capital and he offered me money for the trip—fifteen pesos.

Who was I to argue with destiny? I thanked him for the money, grabbed my clothes and made the trip to Havana, the first stop on my way to beautiful Comiskey Park.

In 1941, he left Perico for good, spent some time playing sandlot baseball while living with his sisters, then returned to the extensive household of Juan Llins. It was in 1943 that Minnie decided to go on his own as a ball player. He had one of his friends write him a letter purporting to be an offer to play baseball in Havana for the Ambrosia Candy team, operated by Rene Midestein. . . Next stop was with Partagas, another semipro nine, and he doubled as a cigar maker. From there, now established as a hard-hitting third baseman, he went to Santiago as player-manager of the Cuban Miners in 1944.

—*Edward Prell, Chicago Tribune Magazine, August 8, 1954.*

Top of the 2nd

I arrived in Havana with, of course, no job and no prospects. I stayed with my sisters and worked for a while in a shoe-shine parlor. A week later I found a job as a carpenter's helper in an orphanage and later became an apprentice brick layer. Destiny was, indeed, elusive. Most of my earnings I gave to my sister, for I needed very little to live on. Within three weeks I returned to El Perico to bring my five-year-old niece, Julita, to Havana. Each day the little girl would wait for me to return home from work and we would go for walks in the parks and to the seashore. Often we would watch the wealthy members of the exclusive Vedado Tennis Club come and go, and enjoy themselves in the magnificent surroundings. It was a status symbol to belong to this Club. It was here where tournaments were held to select the best amateur baseball teams in Cuba, where I longed to one day play in the Amateur Cuban series, one of the great attractions in the world of Hispanic baseball. Many great Cuban stars went to the big leagues from the teams represented here; Sandy Consuegra, Jiqui Moreno, Witto Aloma, Willy Miranda, and many more. The status-conscious Vedado Tennis Club, alas, remained closed to me and many other Cubans, ballplayers and non-ballplayers, because they excluded blacks from membership.

I soon left my brick-laying job and eventually became a houseboy to a wealthy family, a position which caused me much grief. The family would leave from 50 to 100 pesos under the bed or in places I had to clean. I knew they were testing me, to see if I was a thief. I was deeply hurt.

I told the lady of the house this and said that although I was very poor and had come from a humble sugar cane farm, I was not greedy for money. "On the farm," I exclaimed, "no one ever thought I would steal a chicken or a mango even. I had not come to Havana to become a thief." I advised her that I had no intention of taking her pesos and hoped God would give her many more. Furthermore, I told her I was going to become a professional baseball player some day for God had destined me to be so. I guess she thought skinny boys should be seen and not heard for she refused to pay me, arguing that my remarks were offensive. So I quit!

My "break" came when I was seventeen years old. I began work as a cigar maker in the Partagas tobacco factory in Havana. I also, and quite naturally, joined the factory's baseball team. It was a co-ed aggregation and the first baseman was a young girl named Biyaya. I was playing third and during our first practice session when a grounder was hit to me I threw smoothly and softly to first, after all she was "only a girl." Wow, did she get mad. She yelled at the manager that if I didn't throw harder, she would walk off the practice field. On the second ground ball, I threw a little harder, still not full speed. Now she yelled at me. "Throw like you've still got an arm. It looks like you left it at home." Then, the third grounder came my way. Lady, get ready. Ill-tempered, I whipped the ball with all my might. "Go ahead and catch that one!"

She did, and with the greatest of ease. She was a wonder woman, as all those who saw her play will agree. Later, Biyaya, played with an all-girl team in the U.S.

We played against other tobacco company teams with great success. We dominated the league, finished as champions, and I batted .300. One day, Claro Duany, a great ball player then, who now lives in Evanston, Illinois, invited me to practice with the famous Ambrosia Club, the team of a chocolate company. It was a semi-professional team and its manager, Rene Midenstein, told me to play third, then occupied by a twenty-year veteran who boasted nobody had ever replaced him. He retained his position, but I made the team nonetheless.

The first game I played was against El Contreras, and I'll never forget the ninth inning. We were losing and had the bases loaded. Midenstein came over to me and said, "Kid, get in there and bat for Nazario [our left fielder]. Get the hit we need."

The first pitch from Silvio Romero was a smoking fast-ball. I went with the pitch and shot a grounder which bounced off first base and sped to the rightfield fence. Three runs scored and we won the game 3–2. Everyone, not the least of all Orestes Minoso, was elated. I soon became the regular third baseman and that year led the league in batting with a .380 average.

The following year I hit .420, again leading the league. I still held a number of odd jobs—bootblacking, sugar cane harvesting, driving a cart—in order to make enough money to live on. But at eighteen, I decided to permanently settle in Havana and make a career of baseball. I returned to my third base position with Ambrosia.

It wasn't long before I had the opportunity to play outside of Havana. Mario Borroto was putting together some teams to take to the Cuban Mining area in Oriente Province. I was selected for the Cuban Mining team and told I would be paid well for each game. My first game, however, proved to be somewhat a disaster. Hard-throwing Lino Donoso was pitching for the opponents when I came to bat with the bases loaded. An instant replay of what happened with Ambrosia? Not exactly. He struck me out with little effort, we lost the game and I felt terrible. So terrible, in fact, that I told Borroto to send me home.

"Not so fast," he said. There was a second game to be played against another team. Downhearted though I may have been, I stayed around, and a good thing it was. I hit a double and a 380-foot grand slam home run. We won 5-2 and I was a hero.

I went to Borroto and asked him if he wanted me to stay or if I should return to Havana. He thought I was loco; that if I went, the fans would kill him. But I insisted that I owed Rene Midenstein the courtesy of returning because the man had been like a father to me. Borroto called my manager and, characteristically, Rene Midenstein had my best interests at heart. He wished me the best (he called me his protege) and I stayed in Oriente for the next two years, playing for 100 pesos a month. We played top teams, often three times a week and the games always attracted five to ten thousand spectators.

I even managed the team for a few months, but soon gave the job to Tata Solis, who had coached on the team managed by the great Adolfo Luque who had pitched for the Cincinnati Reds in the 1920s. It was Tata who brought me the news that truly changed my life. I remember it as if it were yesterday. It was November 29, 1944 and I was celebrating my birthday in the Placita de Marte in Oriente with a girl friend. We were about to go dancing when Tata ran up waving a telegram. This time it was no hoax.

"Orestes, Orestes," he cried joyfully, "they've taken you for a professional team in Havana. The Marianao want you to try out."

I had a hard time believing it. I knew I had professional ability, and thought a professional team might one day call me. But still it was hard to believe. I grabbed the telegram from Tata. The Marianao team did, indeed, want me to leave for Havana.

"Let's go, Minoso," hollered Tata. "Pull yourself together and go!" What I did next, I still ponder over, still not sure if I did the right and honorable thing. I told Mining team's president, Senor Sent, a good and kind man who had become my friend, that I was really going to Havana to visit a sick sister. I didn't tell him I was going to practice with Marianao. I didn't want to offend him, but he wondered if there was a personal problem. He went so far as to offer me money for the trip, but I told him I had some cash saved up. I really didn't want to tell him why I was going, because if the Marianao didn't sign me, I could return to play with Cuban Mining, and if they *did* sign me, I would call Senor Sent and tell him the truth.

"If you need anything there in Havana, don't fail to call me," were that decent man's parting words.

I asked God to forgive me for this act of deception. I truly believed some lies were of a compassionate nature and this, however it may have seemed, was one.

. . . Minoso was approached by Jorge Pasquel, then grabbing off major leaguers for his Mexican League. Minoso was then getting only $300 a month. . . "Pasquel say, I give you six, seven hunder dolla," Minoso related. "I say no, I no want play Mexico. Pasquel take my arm, go in car. He say, I give you eight hunder. I say no. He open big bag, full money. He say, here take, yours. I say okay, you put all money in Cuba bank and I do." Pasquel refused to go for that and the deal was off. Minoso, having played with others who had been or still were with the Mexican League, had been warned. He explained that the Pasquel contracts seemed to be one-way operations. No matter what the figures were, Pasquel paid what he pleased. Since Pasquel also held the players' passports they were pretty much at his mercy. In any case, Minoso said he didn't want any part of Pasquel. "He got gun, he shoot," he solemnly declared.

—*Herman Goldstein, Cleveland News, April 25, 1949.*

Bottom of the 2nd

La Tropical Park in Havana, surrounded by flower gardens and royal palms, was the home field of the professional Cuban Clubs. Here, I was given a uniform and began taking batting and fielding practice.

The 1944–45 professional season in tropical Cuba began in early December. My Marianao Club was a relatively new entrant in the Cuban League, a circuit which depended for its rivalries on the teams from Cienfuegos, Almendares and Havana. Partisanship was strong in Cuban fans, but none greater than that which existed between the last two teams' faithful. Arguments and even fist-fights were not only common in the stadium where the games were being played but throughout the island where the partisans chanced to meet. And, one must admit, betting heightened this excitement. Not only was betting common on the games, but the "quinielas" were a singularly popular form of betting with the winning ticket indicating the player who first made a hit, scored a run, etc.

While this may have added to the interest and excitement, the partisanship and betting at times made players fear for their physical safety. At the very least, it keep us "looking up." If the fans suspected a player was failing to deliver his best, they would form a "Hungarian Congress" and start pelting the unfortunate athlete with empty beer bottles, seat cushions and whatever else was handy and not nailed down. The guards would then have to intervene, often needing to fire their pistola in the air or even using the flat end of their machete to restore order.

Cuban League games were seldom dull!

There were 30,000 noisy, cheering, betting fans in Tropical Stadium the day I appeared for my first game in a Marianao uniform, wearing number 9, my lucky number which I would carry throughout my career. I remember Daniel Parra was pitching for us against "Professor" Ramon Bragana of Almendares. Unfortunately, I was on the bench and watched as we led 1-0 going into the seventh inning. We were on the field and our third baseman Tony Castano smashed full-speed into the grandstand railing trying to catch a pop foul. He sustained a leg injury that took him out of the game. Our manager, Armando Marsans, looked at me and said, "All right, kid. Go on out there and play third." I was only too happy to oblige.

Almendares tied the score and I came up in the ninth with a man on second and one out. On the first pitch, I hit a low line drive between first and second, scoring the lead run from second. What a thrill! My first time at bat in the Cuban League and I get a tie-breaking it off one of the greatest Cuban pitchers of all time.

In the bottom of the ninth, I threw out two batters on a bunt and ground ball. When I returned to the dugout after the final out, I was hugged and congratulated by my teammates. I'd "made" the team. My dream was fulfilled—I was a professional baseball player.

As I walked out of the stadium and during the bus ride to my sisters' house, people crowded around me, offering their congratulations and encouragement. Suddenly, I was no longer Orestes Minoso, farm worker and semi-pro ball player. I was Orestes Minoso, professional ballplayer of the Marianao Baseball Club. Only a few years ago, I was a kid who looked to professional ballplayers as my idols. Suddenly, I was an idol in the eyes of other young boys. I knew how these kids felt and I always tried from then on to be worthy of their respect. It was a humbling experience. For here I was, seemingly overnight, playing in the same league with men who were my childhood heroes—such stars as Martin Dihingo, Beto Avila, Silvio Garcia, Roberto Ortiz, "Prince" Lazaro Salazar and other. And, now Number 9, Orestes Minoso, was among them.

I was still learning, though. Initially, I swung at any pitch that looked good. And as any player new to the professionals will tell you, you'd better learn to hit the curve ball. I, too, had trouble with the curve ball when I first joined Marianao. I batted in the third position, the same as I was to do in the major league. Although I had great running speed, I wasn't known as a base stealer. In fact, base-stealing was not a widely practiced art in Cuba. We played pretty tight baseball and we could only steal at the orders of the manager. I played third, but it was soon apparent I was out of position. Grounders gave me some trouble and I stopped too many with my chest, relying on my powerful throwing arm to get the man out. I couldn't remotely have equalled the ability of Hector Rodriguez, who played third base for the White Sox in the 1950s and who is regarded as the greatest Cuban third baseman of all time.

I was also fortunate to win my second game in a Marianao uniform with my bat and speed. I beat out a roller to second with the based loaded and the score tied in the ninth. I remember the second baseman, Beto Avila, yelling to me that I ran like a chicken thief. The team's owner immediately called to confirm a contract which payed me 300 pesos a month.

It was about this time that I was offered a lucrative contract to play in the Mexican League. I didn't trust the one making the offer, and besides, I preferred to play in my native Cuba. I even had plans to one day move to the New York Cubans of the Negro Leagues in the United States.

I was told of the discrimination I would have to endure in the U.S. But we had the same in Cuba. An amateur league in Cuba excluded blacks, and other prejudices existed. I always felt that how one reacts to prejudice is what is primarily important.

So I continued playing in Cuba where I finished the Winter League with a batting average of just under .300. I was happy, and the moments memorable. I still remember the day the great American star Dick Sisler smashed three home runs in the same game against my Marianao team. You'll all remember Sisler as the man whose home run against the Dodgers put the Philadelphia Phillies in the 1950 World Series.

I was voted Rookie of the Year and had attracted considerable attention from other baseball organizations, including the New York Cubans and the persistent Mexican League. The choice was mine, playing with Tampico in the Mexican League or the New York Cubans in the American Negro League. The Mexican offer was more substantial, but I couldn't help but think the future of any young professional ballplayer lay in the United States. Besides, I knew of too many good American players, such as Sal Maglie, Lou Klein, Max Lanier and others whose choice of playing in Mexico resulted in setbacks in their careers. Finally, I took my dilemma to my friends at the Partagas tobacco factory where I asked their opinion. Those tobacco buddies of mine voted by banging their work knives on their work tables, voting unanimously in favor of the New York Cubans.

Next stop, Broadway!

The photographs depicting highlights of Minnie's career which follow are credited as follows: (1) Chicago White Sox, (2) Tony Inzerillo, (3) Platon-Athan Studios, (4) National Baseball Hall of Fame, (5) Chicago White Sox, (6) Wide World Photos, Inc., (7) Wide World Photos, Inc., (8) Cleveland Plain Dealer, (9) Wide World Photos, (10) Wide World Photos, Inc., (11) Wide World Photos, Inc., (12) National Baseball Hall of Fame, (13) Cleveland Plain Dealer, (14) Chicago White Sox, (15) National Baseball Hall of Fame, (16) Wide World Photos, Inc., (17) Field Enterprises, Inc., (18) United Press International, Inc., (19) Associated Press.

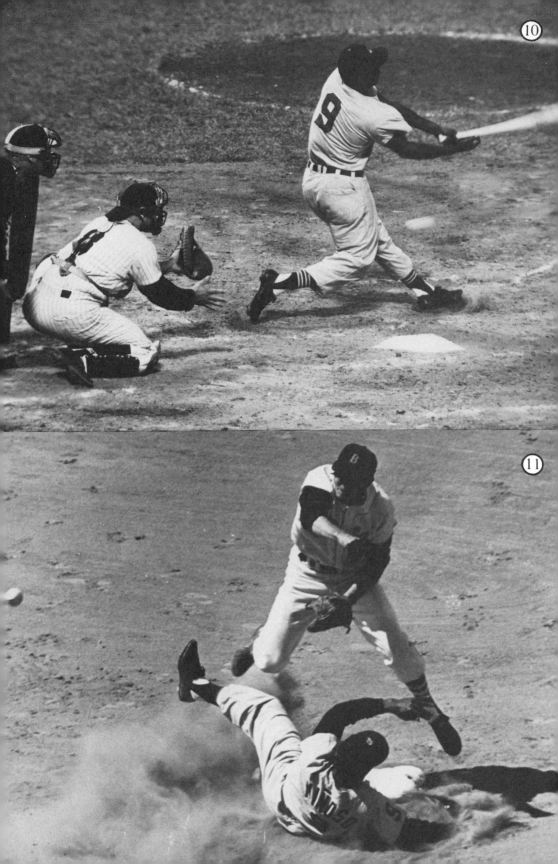

Often described as one of the most exciting players in the game, Minnie's swing shown in the first photo never lost its snap. (2) A smiling Minnie poses after donning Sox uniform once again. (3) Minnie and Al Lopez. (4) The Cuban Comet in action. (5) No fan escapes Minnie's attention. (6) Minnie and Willie Mays at a youth gathering in Chicago. (7) Batting practice in 1954. (8) Safe at third. (9 & 10) A swing and miss against the Yankees, 1958. (11) A good try to break up double play against the Red Sox, 1960. (12) Good for a base hit. (13) He couldn't believe he was in the majors. (14) Didn't anyone ever tell Minnie you shouldn't put soap in a whirlpool?! (15) Another run scored. (16) Front end of a double steal, 1959. (17) Newest member of the Chicago White Sox. (18) Minnie signs in 1952. (19) A natty Minnie, suspended for three days, watches as Indians play Red Sox, 1959.

So Minoso, showing rare judgment in the light of the financial woes which later engulfed the Mexican League and which brought long suspensions to many big leaguers, joined the New York Cubans . . . Minnie kept blasting the ball and there came a day in the summer of 1948 when the Cubans were playing in Birmingham, Ala. "A Cleveland scout come to look at Jose Santiago, our pitcher," Minnie explained. "Jose told him I the best player, that I was in an all-star game in Chicago, but would be in New York in few days. Jose fill out the scout's card with my name. I hit two doubles in New York and the scout sign me."

—*J. G. Taylor Spink, Editor and Publisher, The Sporting News, June 30, 1954.*

I rate him No. 1. I've been around baseball some twenty-three years, and if there's one thing I know, that's a ball player when I see one. He's the fastest. That man's fast as lightning. He's a flat-footed hitter, so he can get anything. You have to keep the ball away from him.

—*Satchel Paige*

Top of the 3rd

I first stepped foot on North American soil in Miami, where my flight from Havana landed. As we touched down, I felt my dream had finally come true. I hurried to catch a train to New Orleans, where the New York Cubans were holding training camp. Along the way, I marvelled at the American farms, the crops I had never seen before and the mechanization which was virtually unknown in Cuba.

We trained and played exhibition games in New Orleans for nearly a month. It should be noted that all the players were already under contract and positioned. Unlike the big leagues, the Negro League did not have second teams or farm teams. Following our final exhibition game, the big moment arrived. We broke camp and headed for New York, the city of skyscrapers I had for so long awaited.

Silvio Garcia and I shared an apartment in a private home near Central Park on 70th Street between 10th and 11th. New York fascinated me—its many stores, cars, well-dressed people, abundant facilities. And, like all tourists, I rode the elevator to the top of the Empire State Building.

Our season began in mid-April, 1945, in the Polo Grounds against the New York Black Yankees. We won 5-2 and, as in my debut with Marianao, I had the good fortune to begin with a flourish. I had two hits, including a home run to right.

I was impressed by the magnificent stadiums in the United States and by their fans. My team's partisans constantly cheered me on, encouraging me to give even more of myself on the field. The fans were further encouraged by our team's success. We had some outstanding players at the time, including catcher Rafael "Ray" Noble who later went on to play with the New York Giants; shortstop Silvio Garcia, pitcher Luis Tiant and many more.

We played over one hundred games that year and finished in fourth place. I was the youngest player on the team and, I must admit, everyone tried to help me, not only to become a better baseball player, but also to learn English. I bought an English/ Spanish dictionary and studied the language of what was to become my adopted country. I became known for hitting to right field, even though I am a right-handed hitter. I played with the New York Cubans for three and a half years, but it wasn't until the third year that I became proficient at stealing bases. When attempting to steal bases, though, speed isn't everything. There's reason to be cautious and to do so only when the opportunity presents itself. Above all, you do not steal on the catcher, but on the pitcher. You observe his every movement, determining exactly when he is going to deliver the pitch or when he is going to whirl and throw to the base.

My salary matched my success at bat and on the bases. From my initial $300 a month, I worked my way up to $1,000 a month in my final season with the Cubans. But money was only part of it. My family had taught me there are greater values than money, and mingling with the great players in the Negro Leagues was an uplifting experience. I was proud and thrilled to appear on the same field with such men as Satchel Paige, Larry Doby, Monty Irvin, Junior Gilliam and literally scores of others. Though I did enjoy some success at the plate, I must admit that I never did get a solid hit off Paige, a confession I know untold other frustrated batters can also make.

I recall one game in the old Polo Grounds. Our Manager Jose Fernandez told Bicho Pedroso, "If you get a hit off Satchel, I'm going to buy you a new Stetson hat." Satchel learned of this promise and vowed that nobody was going to get a hat on him. His team was up by five or six runs and we had two men on base when I came to bat. Bicho hit next. Well, old Satch gave me a base on balls and up came Bicho. Paige hollered in, "Come on, Bicho, come on and bat." He struck the poor fellow out with three lightning fast balls that I'm sure Bicho hardly saw. Striding off the mound, Satchel laughed and yelled, "Bicho, you're not getting any hat at my expense."

Paige was phenomenal. I've never seen another pitcher with as much control. I think he only gave walks when he wanted to, and he always threw his pitches between the waist and the knees, always there are nowhere else. His curve balls were not the great arcs of, say, Camilio Pascual. They were sharp as knives; short, but strong and effective. When Paige figured out a batter's weakness, let's say on an outside corner, that's all the hitter saw from him. Rarely did he lose control. He would not "sell out a pitch," just to get a strike. The batter never knew if he was going to get a curve or a fastball—that was the devilish part about it. One never knew what Paige was going to throw, except that it would probably be in the strike zone and in a place where the hapless batter could not earn his title.

I returned to Cuba to play in the Winter Leagues at the new Cerro stadium. I returned to the Winter Leagues every year until the 1960–61 season, playing a total of fourteen seasons, always with my beloved Marianaos. I averaged .280 and got my share of extra base hits and home runs and, as in the United States, I was renowned for stealing bases and getting hit by pitched balls.

Back in the States, my last year with the Cubans was 1948, the year we won the championship. It was significant in another way, too, for there was now the prospect of making the majors. The year before, Jackie Robinson had broken the "color barrier," and was starring for the Brooklyn Dodgers. Another player, pitcher Jose "Pentalon" Santiago and I were given tryouts with the St. Louis Cardinals, but I didn't remain long in camp. My style of play a third base was criticized: they said I shouldn't throw so hard to first. I couldn't understand why they wanted me to cramp my style, to practice in order to see my stuff. It seemed the Cardinals didn't understand that I was already playing in a strong league and I didn't see why they were making me try out, as if I were some sandlotter. I returned to the Cubans.

When the All-Star games for the Negro Leagues came about, in Chicago and New York, I was told a scout from the Cleveland Indians would be present, looking especially at Santiago and me. His name was Bill Killefer, a former stand-out major league player. He evidently liked what he saw, because he offered the Cubans' owner, Senor Pompei, about $25,000 for signing Santiago and me. I was assigned to their farm team in Dayton and was ready to go, because I realized the minors were a stepping stone to the majors. I appeared in only eleven games with Dayton, but hit .525, with a homer and eight RBI's to my credit.

But I'm getting ahead of my story. Before moving on to Dayton, I was privileged to play in the 1948 World Series of Negro Baseball. We Cubans were the champions of the National League and we played the American League Champion Kansas City Monarchs, led by Satchel Paige. We beat them four games to one and I batted over .300. However, I played unevenly at third base, at times playing as if I created the position and at others making foolish miscues. My performance helped pave the way to the outfield, where I remained for the rest of my baseball career.

Clear the track! The Ebony Limited is heading toward Cleveland Stadium. And it looks like there will be no stopping the Ebony Limited—Orestes Minoso, 23-year-old Cuban Negro—until he lands squarely in the middle of the Indians' lineup. At least that's what Bill Veeck has been hearing from Joe Vosmik, one time Cleveland outfielder, and Bill Killefer, former major league player and manager who now scouts for the tribe. Calling him the fastest thing on legs the game has seen in years, both Vosmik and Killefer are high on the lad and contend he is ready for the majors . . . That's what speed can do for a player. Killefer scouted Minoso when he was playing third base for the New York Cubans of the Negro National League and Vosmik, who will pilot Oklahoma City in the Texas League next year, managed the youngster with the flying heels at Dayton in the Central League . . . Some Dayton fans didn't take kindly to the news that Minoso and Jose Santiago, a pitcher also signed off the Cubans, had been acquired. Several of the regulars, in fact, cancelled their season subscriptions for box seats. But when Orestes got started, they were back begging for a chance to buy their way into the park.

—Ed McFadden, Dayton, Ohio

Bottom of the 3rd

Every black baseball player, every black athlete for that matter, owes Jackie Robinson a genuine debt of gratitude. He showed the way; he endured what many blacks, by temperament, could not. Jackie was a pioneer, a fine human being and a great ball player.

I was the first black player on the Dayton team. I was also one of the *first,* a link in the same chain, supporting our race in both the minor leagues and the majors. I must admit a most sincere gratitude to the fans. Their friendship and kindness were with me from the start. Throughout my career, I tried to respond in the same way. I never felt any really great pressure at being one of the first black players in the major leagues.

That's not to say there weren't some problems. Some of the players were a bit abusive, trying to exasperate me. There was even the major league manager who let loose a small black dog in the stadium where we were playing, trying to draw a comparison with me. I was prepared for this type of "joke," even smiled when I felt it rightfully provoked a reaction. I concentrated on playing ball and, during the game, put aside personal problems.

There are those who say "it was a different game back then; today things just aren't the same." There's an element of truth in what they say. Oh, it's the same game alright, but some aspects have changed radically. Take money, for instance. What baseball player in the late '40s would have thought of a million dollar contract? Even the great Ted Williams received but $125,000 at the top of his career. Today, players with a batting average as low as .240 get much more than that. Also, in those days we had few teams, so many quality players competed for positions. Many sat on the bench who today would be stars. Even Mickey Mantle had to sit it out until Joe DiMaggio retired.

Regulars played when they were hurt because they didn't want to lose their place in the line-up. I was one of them. Even if I sported bandages I asked to play. The large number of teams today are putting more pressure on the minors to come up with players. Consequently, many young athletes are coming to the big leagues before they're ready, sort of like fruit picked before it's ripened. And, might I add, players had no agents. We negotiated our own contracts; owners didn't like to see their players show up with agents or lawyers. Also, players seldom disclosed their salaries. Newspaper writers had to estimate what they were getting.

And while I'm on the subject—I'm just getting warmed up— I've noticed that players today attempt more "spectacular" plays. They throw themselves headlong at balls which usually can be caught without extra effort. Maybe television has something to do with it. Lately, we also see more stolen bases and every team is likely to have a player who weighs about 200 pounds and manages to steal twenty bases each season. I was a three-time champion in stolen bases, with twenty-two, twenty-five and thirty-one steals—and I always weighed about 175 pounds. And there are other differences, such as a player winning a batting title today with a much lower average than formerly, and why a pitcher is considered "good" if he wins fifteen or twenty games, even though his losses are almost equal.

There is no question that .300 hitters are becoming rarer in professional baseball. Is it because more hitters go for the long ball instead of the base hit, as many people seem to think? Or perhaps because of the rise of the relief pitcher to spell a starter who's tiring, even though he is ahead by a comfortable margin? It's a good debate, but one statistic was quite telling. In the mid-fifties, there were only 16 active players with five years or more in the majors who had batting averages of .300 or better, and I was proud to be among them.

Are today's players better than those who played a decade or two ago? Are they worse? It's a question that can't be answered, obviously, because comparisons of this type are always difficult. But in judging the relative merits of the players, statistics aren't always the answer.

During the 1948–49 winter season in Cuba, I received a contract from Cleveland General Manager Hank Greenberg to play for Dayton again the following season. The contract called for the same salary and I asked Greenberg for more. His top offer was $700 a month, and through a translator, I wrote back to him saying I'd just as soon stay in Cuba. This was the first of many holdouts I was involved in, disputes that delayed spring training on a number of occasions. Hank persuaded me to go to Cleveland's camp in Tucson where I batted .400 in exhibition games. My performance must have had the desired effect because I signed a contract for $1,000 a month.

I know I impressed the Indians' brass during spring training not only because of my hitting, but also because of my baserunning. I remember one incident in Texarkana. I was sent in to run for Bob Kennedy who had singled. I moved to second and, in getting ready to deliver his pitch to the next batter, the pitcher whirled and threw to second. He definitely had me picked off, but instead of vainly trying to slide back into the bag I took off for third. It must have startled shortstop Buddy Kerr who took the throw, because he fired the ball to third, was off target, the ball hit me in the neck and I scored.

I came to bat in the eighth inning and hit a home run over the fence in right field. As Manager Lou Boudreau remarked, "Anything can happen now regarding Minoso. He's certainly going to stay with us for some time, maybe for good."

So there I was on the opening day of the 1949 season, playing in the Indians outfield, a member of one of baseball's greatest teams. The Cuban and Negro Leagues were behind me now. A major league career lay before me, and I was determined to make the most of it.

Not that I didn't suffer some set-backs, though.

I stayed with the Indians for about a month, batting only .188, with one home run (during my first game). But I was still a rookie, competing with a number of outstanding outfielders. Even at third base I didn't have a chance. Ken Keltner "owned" the bag, as well he should. The previous year, he hit .297, with 31 home runs and 119 RBIs.

So it was back to the minors. The Indians won the American League flag that year and went on to beat the Boston Braves in the World Series, four games to two. It was a great year for the team's owner, Bill Veeck, a man I could justly call my father in the majors because of the influence he exerted on my career. Cleveland set an attendance record that year with 2,260,627. Always the showman, always the man to give the fans a special thrill, Veeck brought up the great Satchel Paige to pitch in the majors and in the World Series. It was a special moment I know for the forty-one-year-old Satch when he stepped on the mound during the Series. Veeck gave one of baseball's greatest pitchers a chance to perform where he had been denied entrance during his best years. And he also gave a shot in the big leagues to a young sugar cane farmer from Cuba named Saturnino Orestes Arrieta Armas, alias Minnie Minoso. It's something I'll never forget.

Looking at that 1949 Cleveland ballclub, though, it was becoming obvious that I was "in the wrong place at the wrong time." With their lineup, it would be a long time before I made the majors, too long for my satisfaction. I didn't return to Dayton, but was instead assigned to San Diego, a "Triple A" farm club in the old Pacific Coast League. Again, I broke in with a flourish, getting two hits in the first game and as the season went along, keeping my average above .300. That is until we hit Portland and its cool weather. I went two for thirty-two and saw my average plummet to .290. I recuperated in Seattle at the expense of a team managed by Paul Richards. I went four for five in the final game and ended the season with a .297 mark.

San Diego finished fourth in 1949, and during the year I definitely established myself as an outfielder. This was to be my main position, though at times in the majors and later in Mexico I played some third base and even shortstop and first base.

I always felt secure in any ballpark I played in, and not intimidated by the crowds. In fact, the larger the crowd, no matter where I was playing, the more inspired I was. Nonetheless, I learned the hard way that all ball parks are different in some manner, and that if you are going to play well, you must learn to respect those differences.

For example, in San Francisco during the 1949 season, twice, while trying to stop a hit that was going between me and the other outfielder, I managed to play a single into a double. It was very "live" grass causing the ball to bounce very quickly and high. Mistakes like this help to teach one quickly. In a new park, one should get familiar with the ground he's playing on and learn the trajectory of the ball and how best to intercept it.

Another "rookie" blunder made me want to dig the figurative hole and hide in it. I was on third with two out. Our batter smashed a hit and I came home, but because I was too absorbed watching the hit and the runner who was trying for second, I failed to touch home plate. I recall thinking that even if he was called out at second I had scored the winning run. How wrong can a person be. Well, he was out at second, but home plate was still a few feet in front of me because I had stood there watching the play. Obviously, the umpire ruled that no run was scored. I would never forget this embarrassment and throughout my career, the need to hustle at all times was always first on my mind.

The fans love aggressiveness; they come to see hustling players. I tried to live up to their expectations, whether in the field or on the bases, a trait which caused Paul Richards to name me the "Cuban Comet."

I must admit to certain other traits I carried with me during my career, characteristics which were my own—purely Minoso.

When I went to bat, I never liked my teammates to relay signs to indicate what type of pitch it may be. I preferred to determine that for myself. Observing closely, I could usually tell what type of pitch it was when it was a few feet from home plate and I'd make the necessary adjustments. Whether a player is on the field or just warming the bench, he should be aware of everything at all times, and ready to inform his fellow teammates. I was certain to study the opposition and share with my teammates any information which might win the game.

I was always on the lookout for the cheap tricks of baseball, such as the hidden ball trick some players may use to tag out an unsuspecting runner. This flimflam sometimes could mean the difference between winning and losing, or even winning a championship. Players must be aware of the details, because the game is made up of these details. Conscientious, intelligent effort, though not spectacular, can be as rewarding and useful to a team as the play of a superstar noted for raw power and "overwhelming performance."

Courtesy and decency should be exhibited on the playing field. Arguments, bat-throwing and other acts of violence should be avoided. That's not what the people came to see. While I was admittedly not always successful in avoiding arguments, I never reacted violently to the many beanballs which were aimed at my skull. Often, when I was hit by a pitch, I would pick it up and return it to the pitcher in a smooth, underhand motion. Hopefully it would humiliate him. Even when hit I would do this, to let the pitcher know he could not hurt me. Though laughing on the outside, I was often suffering inwardly from being hit. I grant you I did this too often, establishing that unenviable record of being hit by pitches.

Opposing pitchers and managers excused themselves that my style of batting, my "crowding the plate," invited a pitch to hit me. Somehow, I couldn't go along with that line of reasoning, because other hitters who had similar batting styles, and were more of a threat than me, seemed to escape being hit too regularly.

I remember on one occasion when we were playing the Red Sox, I got two quick hits. My third time up, the pitcher nailed me on the back—a very painful blow. I thereupon picked up the ball and tossed it back to the pitcher. He ignored it and went on yelling insults at me while the ball rolled on to center field. I went to first base as if nothing happened. The same pitcher continued hitting me in other games until, with the passing of time, his aggressiveness wore off and finally, one day in Comiskey Park, he apologized to me. He explained that because he was from the Deep South, he took pleasure in hitting me—sort of in revenge. He was more aggravated when I remained calm and serene, smiling and not returning his deliberate attacks and insults. He was sorry also for letting those years go by without having the courage to apologize to me. He asked my forgiveness. When I told him I never felt rancor or sought revenge, he responded, "That's what kills me, your silence, your gentlemanly qualities. You're a great symbol for America."

We shook hands.

But, back to Triple A and my goal to become established as a major league prospect. After the 1949 season I wanted to return, as I always did, to Cuba to play in the Winter Leagues. Hank Greenberg had other ideas. He wanted me to rest instead, in case I became a regular with the Indians. Consequently, I was not able to demonstrate to my Cuban fans how I improved during my stint with San Diego. I was consoled, however, with the hope that I would soon be with the parent club.

Things were different in the following years, though. Major league clubs gave players, principally Latins, the right to play in their native lands during the off season. This I did from 1950 until, as I said, the 1960–61 season.

The winter season's layoff didn't seem to affect me, however, when I returned to San Diego the following season. I suppose when one is younger, a long inactive period doesn't affect him as it does an older person. Even during my leisure, I managed to maintain my playing weight of 175 pounds, and I do to this day. This fact may make many weight-watchers angry, or at least a bit envious, because I love pastas, cakes, potatoes, steaks and, of course, the Hispanic specialty supreme, paella, a combination of seafood, rice, squid, peppers and saffron. Furthermore, I love to cook and, all modesty aside, admit to being somewhat of a gourmet chef. Many men of Spanish heritage are excellent cooks, taking pride in their creations. Hopefully, this should help dispel the myth that the typical Hispanic male is a macho-tyrant who sits around waiting for the woman of the house to bring him his food. And, if I may make one more gastronomical observation before returning to baseball—the "taco syndrome," so popular in the United States, is not traditionally Spanish by any stretch of the imagination. It's merely an improvisation that the poor have learned to flavor their meager rations and to give them gusto.

When I arrived in the Indians' spring training camp in Tucson, I actually thought I had a good chance to make the team. I was more confident because general manager Greenberg seemed to have indicated that I had such an opportunity. Though I thought I did well, I was assigned again to San Diego. Greenberg had sent me a contract in Cuba that winter, but I didn't sign it. Finally, we agreed to $1,600 a month and off to San Diego I went. Cleveland still seemed elusive, notwithstanding the fact that they finished fourth in 1950 behind New York, Detroit and Boston. In the World Series that year, the Yanks, under Casey Stengel, KO'd the Phillies in four straight. The Indians still had a host of stars, and breaking into the lineup would be difficult. I now looked to 1951, and though I didn't know it then, it would be the turning point of my life—the majors.

I first met Minnie Minoso in San Francisco. I had heard that
Minoso had a lot a of trouble with the English language.
People said he couldn't speak a word of it. I went over to him,
shook hands, and told him that we were happy to have him
with our team. I told him about the team, baseball in the
Pacific Coast League, and so on. Minoso didn't say a word.
Then, I asked him: "Do we owe you anything for expenses?"
'Expenses?' he asked. 'Yes' Then he rattled off a list: Hotel
expenses, transportation, meals, tips. I was surprised. He
really understood what I was talking about when
I mentioned money!

—*Bill Starr, President of the San Diego Padres, 1950.*

It begins to appear now that Minnie the Masher will stick.
Minnie is Orestes Minoso and his nickname has nothing to do
with *amour toujours*. It's a nickname the Indians have given
him for his savage bat swinging. "Anything can happen now
regarding Minoso," says Lou Boudreau. "He certainly is going
to stay with us for some time, maybe for good." Minnie's
progress as an Indian now is being compared with the rapid
rise of Larry Doby. Only there are many who believe he will get
there faster. Unlike Doby, he isn't sensitive and easily wounded
by such things as cab drivers in Texarkana refusing to pick up
the Negroes yesterday. Minnie's a native of Cuba. There isn't
as much difference in pigmentation there, and the social
problems are lighter. He's as free as a blackbird
and flies like a deer.

Frank Gibbons, Press Staff Writer, April 12, 1949.

Top of the 4th

During the 1950 season in San Diego I did my best to live up to major league expectations. San Diego always looked like a small city to me, or better yet, a big city with a small population. Their fans were enthusiastic and 100 percent behind their Padres. The team's home stadium was not the same one used by the present day Padres of the National League. The fences were shorter and it accommodated only 15,000 spectators. But those in attendance made it look bigger by waving banners and shouting their approval for our aggressive play. The stadium reminded me of Cerro Stadium in Havana, site of my first major triumph. Even though I had confidence in myself, the cheers and applause of the fans gave me more will and fortitude and, as we used to say in Cuba, to "Eat the ball!"

I remember that one day, about a month before the season ended, Hank Greenberg showed up at the ballpark, donned a uniform and began taking practice with us. He was surprised to see me playing shortstop, and doing quite well, I might add. I was competing for the batting championship that year, looking forward to my best season ever. He noticed I avoided him and came over to me to ask if I had a problem. I told him I didn't have anything to say to him, told him I couldn't afford to buy Christmas presents for my family that year because I wasn't allowed to play in Cuba during the winter and furthermore I was still here and not with the Indians as I was led to believe I might have been. All the while I was looking around for someone to translate what I was saying.

I was becoming more aware that I didn't fit into Cleveland's plans. When he said I was still Cleveland property, I replied that it didn't much matter one way or the other. I thereupon took leave of the general manager and repaired to the locker room, aware that any negotiation with Cleveland was now out of the question. Deep down, in spite of this disagreeable incident, I sympathized with Hank. He had been one of my idols and still was. In time we became very strong friends. I thought I was being treated unfairly, but I realize now that Greenberg, always the perfect gentleman, had a job to do.

I had a great year in San Diego. I played in 169 games, the most I ever played in one season, both in the outfield and at shortstop. I hit .339, rapped out 203 hits, batted in 115 runs and hit 20 homers. It was a fitting farewell to San Diego and its wonderful fans.

I returned to Havana, and was granted permission to play winter ball. I hit .321 that season in my native land and received the praise of the fans, baseball-crazy Cubans who also cheered other Cuban ballplayers who were making it big as stars in the majors: Pascual, Ramos, Consuegra, Miranda, Aloma and others. Politics and baseball were the "daily bread" on the island and the exploits of Cuban baseball players were headline news events. I was proud to be doing my share as the years went by to raise the Cuban flag high in the United States.

Again, in the spring of 1951, I returned to the Indians' spring training camp in Tucson with high hopes. After we broke camp, I went with the team and during an exhibition game Manager Al Lopez called me over and asked if I'd ever played first base. I answered "no" but that I'd be willing to try. "Okay," said Lopez, you'll bat for Clark next time he's due up. Well, the bases were loaded when Clark's turn finally came and I pinch-hit for him. I swung and the ball sailed over the right field fence, and I was the regular first baseman for the rest of the exhibition season. At long last, I was with the Indians.

We opened the season in Detroit. Bob Lemon was our starting pitcher and in the seventh inning I substituted for Luke Easter at first. I remained there and fit quite well, I thought, into the team's plans.

It was nearing the end of April and time for the teams to begin reducing their rosters to the required number of men. Because of my play, I knew I wouldn't be sent down. It was April 30, 1951, and we were in St. Louis to play the Browns in a double-header. I went four for four in the opener and three for four in the night-cap. Afterwards, in the locker room I was happy and content. I looked up at Al Lopez as he approached my locker. Laconically, the man they call "Senor" told me, "Minnie, you've been traded to the Chicago White Sox."

I felt my world had collapsed, I just clammed up and on the train that night, I locked myself in my private compartment and didn't respond to any of the several knocks from my teammates and friends. I felt down and dismayed. I didn't know where my future lay.

I couldn't keep back the tears. "If I was well known in Cleveland and had made friends, what's going to happen to me with the White Sox where I don't know anybody?" I genuinely worried how I would be accepted...the first black player on the team.

There was more knocking at the door and I heard our star third baseman Ray Boone pleading for me to let him in. Still in tears, I opened the door. "Look, Minnie," he began, in a consoling voice, "everything will be okay in Chicago. You're a great player, but in Cleveland, you'd never play regularly. Chicago has great fans, and they appreciate good ballplayers." Boone's words put my mind at ease and after he left I was able to sleep the rest of the way from St. Louis to Cleveland.

The next day I went immediately to get my belongings from the clubhouse, ignoring a request from Hank Greenberg to see him. He insisted and I finally agreed. I said it wasn't necessary to explain the trade. I believed the primary reason was because Cleveland already had several black players and I was expendable. I had to resign myself to the situation.

The reasons for the trade, I learned later, were quite different from my initial views. The number of blacks on the roster was immaterial. Manager Lopez wanted to strengthen his chances to win the pennant and to do so he needed a left-handed pitcher. Thus, on April 30 the Indians became involved in a three-team trade. I went to the White Sox while two of my teammates, pitcher Sam Zoldak and catcher Ray Murray were sent to the Philadelphia Athletics. In return, the Indians received left-hander Lou Brissie, a top pitcher and war hero who had sustained almost crippling injuries on the battlefield. The Athletics also traded outfielder Paul Lehner to Chicago while the White Sox sent Dave Philley and hard-hitting outfielder Gus Zernial to Philadelphia. Each team hoped they had strengthened themselves, for each was hungry for a pennant. Although Cleveland was the World Series champion in 1948, the Athletics hadn't won the American League flag since 1931, and the White Sox had to look all the way back to 1919 for their last pennant, and that tainted by the "Black Sox" scandal. Each team needed help.

In 1950, the Indians finished fourth, the Sox sixth and the Athletics eighth and last. It was also the final year of managing for the immortal Connie Mack—in 1951, Jimmy Dykes became the A's new manager.

The White Sox also got a new manager in 1951, a man who was to exercise significant influence on my baseball career: Paul Richards. And so it was that I arrived on Chicago's great south side, an area about which I knew next to nothing. What I did understand was that Chicago fans knew their baseball and that they were demanding. This didn't bother me a bit; quite obviously, I welcomed the challenge. These fans wanted a pennant. The last Chicago World Series was in 1945, but that involved the Cubs, the northside team, a part of town that might have just as well been on another planet as far as the Comiskey Park faithful were concerned.

I realized when I arrived at the magnificent, historic park at 35th and Shields that it was imperative that I play ball the very best I knew how. I had no idea how long it would be before I would be able to capture the hearts of the White Sox fans.

Minoso's fast. He's safe on an error. He's safe on ground balls that should be double plays. He scores on short flies. He's safe going from first to home. All those things average up. All those things beat you.

—*Casey Stengel, June, 1951*

"I'm tickled to death...!" The words came from Orestes (Minnie) Minoso, brilliant freshman outfielder-third baseman of the Chicago White Sox. Ever since he was notified of his selection as Rookie of the Year in the American League by the THE SPORTING NEWS, there hasn't been a happier person in Cuba—or for that matter, anywhere. Minnie, when he learned of his selection said: "When you go to the Big Show, you know you are receiving the chance of your life. And you know you've got to make the best of it. And making good isn't as easy as many people think. You gotta work hard, be on your toes all the time and meet all kinds of challenges."

—*Pedro Galiana, Havana, Cuba for The Sporting News, December 12, 1951.*

Minoso is what Manager Richards has described as a "natural" player. "He literally lives the game," says the lean, wise White Sox pilot. "I doubt if he ever knew about or cared about anything else. He's learned about money now, but I doubt if that will make any difference in the exemplary life he leads. It may only stimulate his intense interest in making good. He does everything well on the field. He can run, throw, hit, think, and he can play any position. You can put him anywhere on the field and forget about him. He knows the score at all times. There is no type of pitching which bothers him, or if it does, it doesn't bother him long."

—*John C. Hoffman, Baseball Digest, October 1951.*

Bottom of the 4th

I arrived on the "Destiny Express," the nickname I gave the train which brought me to Chicago from Cleveland. I moved in with the Lewis family, old friends, who lived in the neighborhood of 63rd and Maryland. The following day I took a cab to Comiskey Park, arriving at 11AM, just before batting practice. I learned later that Manager Richards had called a club meeting before my arrival, announcing that the Sox were going to have a black ballplayer for the first time. Personally, he said, he didn't care what a player's skin color was, but asked if anyone on the team had any personal problems in the matter. No one raised his hand.

The White Sox that year were a team with a nucleus of outstanding baseball players, a team which it was clear to see would one day challenge for the league championship. The 1951 Sox had Eddie Robinson, Nellie Fox, Chico Carrasquel, Bob Dillinger, Al Zarilla, Jim Busby, Phil Masi, Bud Stewart, Floyd Baker, Gus Niarhos and a host of fine pitchers: Billy Pierce (who became one of the finest left-handers in the history of the game), Saul Rogovin, Ken Holcombe and my compatriot, Luis Aloma.

It was a memorable Tuesday afternoon when I made my debut in a White Sox uniform, wearing as usual my lucky number 9. I started in left field before a packed house, as was expected, because the fans were full of curiosity. I was probably the first black Cuban most of them had ever seen. Richards placed me third in the batting order, my favorite position.

In a very few minutes, I was to enjoy one of my greatest thrills in baseball. In a split second, a bond was tied between the White Sox fans and Minnie Minoso which has to this day remained unbroken, a bond I pray will always be strong.

We were playing the Yankees that unforgettable afternoon in the "Old Roman's" ball park. Vic Raschi was the New York pitcher, one of the best in the American League. The previous season he had a 21-8 record for the world champs and was on his way to another outstanding year. I came up to the plate for the first time with Don Lenhardt on first and one out. I had closely observed Raschi's gestures and movements and approached the plate in my usual leisurely style. I remember what happened next as if it were yesterday. Raschi came in with a high slider. I swung at it with enthusiasm. And I connected! Running to first, I watched as the ball sailed over the centerfield fence, 450 feet away. Comiskey Park erupted as I had never seen a baseball stadium before. As I rounded the bases, I hoped in my heart that I was here to stay. We won 4-2, my two-run blast being the margin of victory. Could any player ask for more in his first game in a new city?

I was filled with joy that day. I wondered how my family and friends in Cuba felt because I knew radio broadcasts told them of my good fortune. Did I finally have a secure place with one ballclub? I felt my abilities were sufficient to have earned a starting spot and that I could develop these skills to the maximum. I also felt lucky to have Paul Richards as a manager. He was a serious man who nonetheless possessed a dry wit, a man whose practical intelligence enabled him to manage a team with extraordinary success. He knew how to mold ballplayers and treated each one of us with kindness and appreciation.

He was always ready to help a player overcome a problem, and had a knack for knowing just what to do to help a player achieve his potential. Take the case of our fine shortstop, Chico Carrasquel. Chico was one of the slickest fielding shortstops in baseball, but had trouble at the plate, especially with the curve ball. He had the habit of sticking his left foot behind him when he was about to stride into a pitch. Richards corrected this by tying a rope around his waist and left leg. He made it long enough so he could hold on to it. Then when Chico was ready to move his left leg, the skipper pulled the rope firmly to stop his movement. It took a good amount of practice, but Richards was finally able to correct the Venezuelan's problem, and Chico was able to cope with the curve ball better.

Richards was also extremely successful with pitchers, time and again helping them become winners. My teammate and fellow-Cuban Sandy Consuegra was an early beneficiary of Richards' talent.

He was spiked in Tampa during a spring training game in 1954. Twelve stiches were needed to close the wound and the following day when Richards asked for him he was told Consuegra was resting in his hotel room. The skipper told the team masseur to bring Sandy to the ballpark, and in due course the young Cuban arrived, justifiably puzzled. His teammates shared his bewilderment, especially when Richards told him to go put on his uniform. So, Sandy limped to the dressing room as we all wondered what the manager, ingenious as he was, could possibly do with an injured ballplayer. Sandy limped back, attired in his uniform and wearing one spiked shoe and a sandal on his injured foot. "Bring me two boards, two posts and some rope," ordered Richards.

He ordered Sandy to warm up for about 15 or 30 minutes. Sandy thought Richards was crazy, but I advised him the manager knew what he was doing and it was for Sandy's own good. In all the confusion, who among us would have thought that Richards and the park workers were going to build a swing. Well, he did build one and told the confused Consuegra to climb in it and begin throwing pitches to the catcher. To everyone's surprise, the contraption actually worked. Even Sandy admitted it.

But *why* was an excellent question. Richards explained that he wanted Sandy's muscles to remain strong, especially his pitching arm. Consuegra, Richards knew, had to perfect his

control as well as work on a variety of pitches. The exercise also
was added insurance against weight gain. Consuegra used the
improvised swing for fifteen days and kept in shape for the
1954 season. Did it work to his advantage? It just so happened
that 1954 was Sandy's best year in the majors as he posted a 16-3
mark, thus becoming the American League's top pitcher.

It was incidents such as these which made the Chicago White
Sox of the 1950s, led by Paul Richards, one of the most exciting
and innovative teams in the major league baseball.

But back to Minoso and his growing affection for the city of
Chicago and its wonderful fans.

There's no question that I enjoyed getting the decisive hit or
making the game-saving catch that helped us win the game. The
success of the team, however, always came first. Likewise, I was
always upset when I made an error that cost runs to be scored
against us or, worse, lost the game. Quite frankly, I'll never forget the errors I made that spring. All too many of them were at
third base, where I was often stationed. In one unforgettable
game against the Yankees, I made one error at third and another
in left field. The latter was caused by using the wrong glove and
letting a line drive get by. Afterwards, Sox general manager
Frank Lane presented me with a special mitt. I keep it as one of
my fondest memories of my early days with the White Sox.

Lane paid me a fine compliment in one newspaper interview
when he was asked to comment on the trade which brought me
to the White Sox. "Richards, who managed at Seattle last year
knew all about Minoso and Henry Simpson. He felt that Simpson had a future but Minoso was the man for us and our 1951
urgency. In view of what Minoso has done and Simpson has yet
to accomplish, I do not blame Cleveland for being chagrined."

Although I seemed to make more than my share of errors, my
batting was consistently high during the first games with the
Sox. The more I played, the more confidence I gained. And the
vocal appreciation of the fans helped spur me on. As time went
by, I played more and more in left field, although there were
times when I was put in right for a play when a hard-hitting left-
handed batter came to the plate in a critical situation. After he
was disposed of, I moved back to the left—yet another innova-

tion of manager Richards. On a few occasions, I even played shortstop and first base. As a boy in Cuba, remember, I learned to play all nine positions. In Cuba, I even switch-hit sometimes, but never felt really comfortable as a left-handed hitter. I was always afraid of striking out.

One strange statistic needs mentioning here. As a newcomer to the big leagues, my average showed I was more effective against right-handed pitchers than left-handers. I hit .360 against right-handers compared to a meagre .200 against left-handers. This against all the odds which showed that right-handed hitters hit left-handed pitchers better, and vice-versa. But, then, Minoso always had to be different.

As the 1951 season wore on, I was gaining a reputation as a base stealer. Richards realized how this ability would help the Sox win games and often gave me the green light; in other words if you think you can steal the base, go ahead and give it a try. It was about this time that he dropped the name "Cuban Comet" on me. My base stealing and general speed on the basepaths soon brought the chant from the stands of "Go, Minnie, Go!" whenever I reached base. I like to think this helped the entire team to be known as the "Go, Go White Sox," for I wasn't the only speedster on the team. The 1950s had such great baserunners as Jim Busby, Hector Rodriquez, Chico Carrasquel, "Jungle Jim" Rivera, Nellie Fox, and later the great Luis Aparicio, who helped bring about this "Go, Go" spirit of what I consider one of the greatest and certainly most exciting teams in baseball history.

During that first year with the Sox I established myself early as a base-stealing threat and daring runner. By mid-June, I had 10 stolen bases and teammate Jim Busby had 14 to lead the league. I often stretched singles into doubles and took second on what would normally be a one-base fielding error. This baserunning caused the following comment from pitcher Billy Pierce when asked who would steal more bases during the year, Busby or me. He answered it would be Busby, because "Minnie won't get as many chances to steal because he never stops at first base."

I recall a game against the Indians. I lifted a weak pop fly to

Ray Boone at third. Somehow Ray muffed it for an error. By the time he recovered I was sliding into second base well ahead of his throw to George Stirnweiss.

As my friend Bill Veeck said after the game, "I love to watch him (meaning me) play. He'll give you a thrill every game."

As for my base-running, Paul Richards told Edgar Munzel of the *Sun Times,* "You know, I have found that Minoso uses excellent judgment in his running. He has yet to try to stretch a hit or score on a fly ball and not make it. He differs in that respect from almost every other spectacular base runner of his type. Almost invariably they start getting reckless and run into suicide."

In fact, my baserunning and that of teammate Jim Busby in the early '50s inspired one fan to write to Richards and advise that if Jim and I were ever on first and second with less than two out, Paul should signal the squeeze bunt and see if both of us could score.

I would like to caution you on one point, though. I did not run the bases, as has been suggested on occasion, with reckless abandon. I ran them according to plan; not on wild impulse. Let's say I was a strategic runner, a learned quality that truly educated me in the art of base stealing. I learned how to study the pitcher and catcher, and how to fake my actions seemingly with every pitch. Rarely, did I reach first base with the intention of stealing second base immediately. Instead, I'd study the pitcher's movements, for as I said previously, a runner generally steals on the pitcher, not the catcher. Then, if I had Richard's "green light," I'd make the decision of whether to take off. The inspiring "Go, Go" chant of the fans would have you believe I could steal second whenever I wanted. Obviously, this was not the case. I wasn't sure all my attempts would work, but when I did commit myself, I'd roar full speed to the bag and slide— always slide. Even when I was racing to a bag I wasn't stealing I usually slid into it. This may have given me the dirtiest and most torn uniform in the league, but I believe it also saved me from sustaining serious injury. Sliding prevented me from twisting or breaking my ankles, suffering knee injuries and tendon pulls and getting "charlie horses." It's my belief that when runners reach a base at full speed, and then pull up quickly without slid-ing, they invite the injuries mentioned above, sort of like a car that is braked while traveling at a fast rate of speed. If you slide into a base, the worse you can get is a minor scrape. And, by all means, once you commit yourself to slide, by all means slide. A change of heart at the last moment could be serious. When one becomes a professional slider, you'll be able to slide even on concrete.

That first year I remember especially the wild enthusiasm the Sox fans exhibited when we returned to Chicago after a road tour during which we won fifteen games in a row. Somehow, I was credited with inspiring this success, and "Go, Minnie, Go" resounded from the stands at 35th and Shields. "As Minoso goes, so go the Sox," was a popular, if somewhat romanticized, assessment of our success. While I appreciated the sentiment, there were twenty-four other guys on the team who deserved equal billing. *We* were on the move. It was a long time since the Chicago White Sox were a first division team, and a serious contender for the American League flag. Although I was just a rookie, I tried not to let all the nice things the sports writers said about me go to my head. I do recall most fondly, though, what Bill Veeck said about me. "I don't believe there is a player in the game today who can give you the thrill he can. Without him in the lineup, it's just another ball game."

Kind and generous words from a very kind and generous man.

Sometimes this rapport could get a bit out of hand. Take the time when the good people at the Packinghouse Workers Hall on south Wabash threw a dance in my honor. Well, it seems things got somewhat rowdy and the police had to put an emer-gency plan two into effect when the crowd estimated at over 3,000 overflowed into the street. About five squad cars and 15 officers responded to control traffic which, understandably, moved slowly through the area. I soon learned there was no beating a good time on Chicago's great southside.

The crowds at Comiskey Park grew, and special police details struggled to control them. I can still hear those enthusiastic

fans, so hungry for a pennant, stomping, clapping and shouting, "Go, Minnie, Go!"

That fifteen-game winning streak, though, led many fans to
believe that 1951 was going to be a championship year. Unfortunately, as so often happens with teams, we had our ups and
downs and finished with a record of eighty-one wins and
seventy-three losses, good for fourth place, and first division.
Though this may appear as somewhat of a modest finish, one
must remember that White Sox fans hadn't had a first division
team to cheer for years. They loved our aggresive play and during the season we could at any time become, as we would say in
Spanish, "a monster-mash," and beat anybody. We were especially potent at Comiskey Park and teams would save their best
pitchers to oppose us when they arrived in town. Also, as we
used to say in Cuba, "a baseball is a capricious object, because
even though it comes in a square box, it is round." This capri-
ciousness was mysteriously demonstrated by realizing that a
club which gave us the most trouble was the St. Louis Browns,
the last place team in 1951. Who can forget the St. Louis
Browns? They were the butt of many a joke and are a favorite
subject of Bill Veeck's speeches; for Veeck had the dubious
honor of owning the team for a while during the 1940s.

It was the Brown's pitching which gave us the most trouble.
Although they were a last place team, they still had some fine
hurlers. Their best was Ned Garver who led the league in 1951
with a 20-12 mark. They also had Duane Pillette, Jim Mc-
Donald, Tommy Byrne and the old man himself, Satchel Paige.
We found it hard to outsmart them, and they were especially
rough on us in St. Louis.

The year 1951 will always be memorable to me, not only because it was my rookie year. It was also a great year for baseball. It was the year of the miracle finish by the New York
Giants in the National League, capped by Bobby Thomson's
home run against the Dodgers that put Leo Durocher's charges
in the World Series against the Yanks. Casey Stengel's team beat
the Giants four games to two that year, a year that saw Joe Di-

Maggio say goodbye to baseball and a year which saw Ford Frick replace "Happy" Chandler as commissioner of baseball. It was the year a rookie by the name of Mickey Mantle first appeared in a Yankee uniform and the year four Cleveland pitchers, Bob Feller, Mike Garcia, Bob Lemon and Early Wynn, combined to grab more than eighty victories. They were super pitchers to be sure, but I'm proud to state that against those four standouts I batted .360 that year. My success against Bob Feller's 98-mile-per-hour fastball can be summed up by saying I just didn't go after it with a home run swing. I watched his movements closely and swung to meet the ball. With his speed, mere contact with the ball will drive it a long distance.

During 1951, I vied for the batting title with the great Ferris Fain of the Athletics. Fain eventually won it with a .344 average and I finished at .326. In my battle with him I remember one particular game against the A's. Fain was hitting over .330 at the time and went hitless his first two times at bat. His third time up, he socked a deep fly to right which our outfielder pulled down about two feet from the fence. Angry, Fain kicked the first base bag and fractured a toe, disabling him for a month.

Another amusing moment occurred when the Washington Senators visited town. Their pitching squad included my fellow countrymen Julio "Jiqui" Moreno, Connie Marrero and Consuegra, soon to be a White Sox. I hollered out to them that if they threw Fain "rockets" in the next A's-Senators series and got him out I'd buy them all dinner. So what happened? Fain rapped out seven hits in a double-header against the Senators and pushed his average over .340, leaving me back in the dust. I never let those guys forget it—some countrymen! It was all in fun, of course, and I knew what they meant when they said that Fain hit them with "the tip of the axe," for Fain was one of the top hitters of the decade.

I wasn't the only Sox player who hit over .300 that year. Nellie Fox batted .313 and Bob Dillinger finished with a .301 mark. Eddie Robinson hit twenty-nine home runs and fleet-footed centerfielder Jim Busby had twenty-six steals. Personally, 1951 was one of the most rewarding years I've ever had in baseball, mainly because I did so well as a rookie, proving that I was an authentic major leaguer. In addition to my .326 batting average, I rapped out 173 hits: 34 doubles, 14 triples and 10 home runs. I batted in 76 runs and scored 112. Of tremendous satisfaction, though, was that I led the league in stolen bases with 31.

The year 1951 also witnessed the beginning of a "habit," the habit of getting hit by pitched balls. I recall one doubleheader in particular with the Athletics, when I was low-bridged a number of times. How many of these were caused because of my "crowding the plate" is, of course open to debate. I was nicked with pitches once in each game, but the aim of the A's pitchers was bad enough for me to get out of the way the rest of the day. I responded in the best way I knew—I got ten hits in twenty-two times at bat for the entire five-game series with Philadelphia and in that twin-bill had five hits, two rbi's and two stolen bases.

I soon made it a point to always wear the protective headgear. I even told one sportswriter that I was going to wear it to bed in case they come and try to hit me when I'm sleeping.

One of the most exciting episodes in the 1951 season involved selection of the American League's Rookie of the Year. It was generally considered that Yankee second baseman Gil Mc-Dougald and I were the leading contenders. After the year ended, the poll was taken and the Baseball Writers Association of America awarded the honor to McDougald. Indignation, especially in Chicago, arose. Sox general manager Frank Lane said, not only of McDougald's selection, but of Yogi Berra being named Most Valuable Player in the American League: "It seems you must play on a pennant winner to earn these honors. If that's the way they are picked, both awards might as well be abandoned. It wasn't his (Minnie's) fault that he wasn't on a pennant winner. He's my Rookie of the Year regardless of how the baseball writers voted. As a matter of fact, Minoso, in my estimation, was the Most Valuable Player in the league. It certainly wasn't Berra."

Statistics tend to indicate that Lane had a point. While Mc-Dougald was a tremendous ball player and certainly went on to stardom with the Yanks, my numbers were better. For example—hits: McDougald, 123; Minoso, 173; total bases: Mc-Dougald, 196; Minoso, 265; triples: McDougald, 4; Minoso, 14; batting: McDougald, 306; Minoso, 326; RBIs: McDougald, 63; Minoso, 72. I also led him in being hit by pitches, 16-4, but then I was always tops in that department.

Incidentally, the National Rookie of the Year was 20-year-old Willie Mays.

The thrills and honors of 1951, though, more than compensated for not being Rookie of the Year. Actually the *Sporting News* did accord me that title.

Memorable moments? I recall a game in Fenway Park against the Red Sox. I was on third and our batter hit a soft-fly to short centerfield. Dom DiMaggio raced in to catch it, and I tagged up. Third base coach Jimmy Adair yelled, "No, Minnie, No!" "It's too late," I answered. Dom caught the ball and I shot like a bullet toward the plate. Dom hurled the ball home and I slid. I can see it now—the ball bounced into the catcher's mit, he lunged at me and the umpire called "safe!" The run was our margin of victory.

We next traveled to Yankee Stadium and, by coincidence, the same situation arose. This time, Dom's older brother, Joe, ran in to snare the pop fly. I tagged and faked a rush for the plate. I watched as the throw came in and heard DiMaggio yell to me, "Hey Minnie. See if you can beat me the way you beat my brother in Boston." What I did in Boston, though, was in a moment of inspiration. I wasn't about to test the Yankee Clipper. Good thing, too, because the throw he made was right on the money and I'd have been out.

I do remember, though, burning the Yankees. I scored from third base on a pop-up just beyond the infield. The ball was caught by Gil McDougald, who was unable to throw me out.

The year 1951 was, indeed, a year of surprises. One I'll remember always was Minnie Minoso Day at Comiskey Park.

The date was September 23 and we were playing the Browns. None other than Satchel Paige was scheduled to pitch. A group of southside black citizens promoted the day and stood next to me at home plate as the tribute was offered. I was grateful for this attention and for the many gifts they showered upon me, including a television set, radios, cameras and a brand new Packard. I was even presented with the deed to a newly-constructed apartment as a sign of appreciation from the leading businessmen of that area. This appreciation was for living in their community and for the fact, they said, that my popularity helped bring people into their places of business.

I was especially pleased at the response my play received from the youngsters. I always tried to accommodate them by signing autographs whenever possible. Sometimes there would be literally hundreds milling around me before and after games at Comiskey Park. Let's face it, they were spoiling me, and I loved it. I appreciated their feelings and was proud to be their hero, for I've never forgotten how, as a young boy in Cuba, I looked up to ballplayers. Sometimes the police would worry about the tumult, but I never tired of meeting the youngsters and signing scorecards, balls, notebooks and whatever else they gave me. I tried never to refuse them and I haven't regretted those occasions. It fills me with pride when now I meet adults who show me souvenir autographs I signed twenty-five years ago. Seeing these remind me of those happy days in the early 1950s when the White Sox were truly a team "on the go." I'm always pleased to provide these fans with another signature, my contemporary one.

I always enjoyed particularly good relations with the members of the Chicago press corps. I especially was on good terms with the late Bob Elson, the Sox radio commentator. We all admired him, not only because of his superb knowledge of the game, but also because he was such a gentleman. Bob made us all feel at ease with him.

While I, least of all, should find fault with the press—they did give me outstanding publicity from my first day in a Sox uniform—there are players whom they tend to overlook on occasion. For instance, Roberto Clemente, who went virtually unnoticed in his early years though he was one of the most talented players in baseball. It wasn't until the World Series of 1960, when he led his Pirates to victory over the Yanks, that he was really "discovered."

My success in baseball enabled me to meet and become friends with many sports and entertainment stars. I was fortunate enough to meet vocalist Sarah Vaughan while she was performing in Chicago. I also became great friends with Joe Louis, a fine gentleman. He was a professional in and out of the ring and his willingness to share with the poor is well known. Another friendship I will forever treasure was with Nat King Cole. Often would he come to the ballpark to watch me play. When he debuted at the famous Tropicana night club in Cuba, I had the pleasure of attending. To my astonishment, he dedicated his performance to me. With the audience rising in applause and my friend Nat standing there, I thought I'd burst with emotion. I still have a photograph taken at that performance. To me it is priceless.

I also have fond memories of George Shearing, June Christy, Duke Ellington, Louis Armstrong and others, mainly because of my natural love for music and dancing.

Before I return to baseball, I must relate one incident my friends and I still talk about. I like Chinese food and whenever in Boston—Chico Carrasquel, Luis Aloma, Mike Fornieles, Sandy Consuegra, and whoever else was free joined me at one particular Chinese restaurant. The manager always set aside a special table for us and prepared a generous menu for each occasion. On one visit, I wondered why the waiters were huddled together, whispering and glancing at me from time to time. Later I learned that they were astonished to see a black man handle chop sticks so well.

I was a big leaguer, looking forward to the 1952 season. I was aware that I'd reached my peak and also aware of my debt to my adopted country, the United States. While I was, indeed, proud to become a United States citizen, I still retained feelings of compassion for Cuba and other Latin American countries. It has always been my hope for other Hispanics to have the same opportunities for success in the big leagues as I had. I was pleased, therefore, to note the rise of players whose success brought honor to Latin America—Valdivielso, Ramos, Marrero, Consuegra, Pascual, Taylor, Cuellar, Tartabull, Oliva, Clemente, Rivera, Amoros, Aparicio, Marichal, the Alous, Pagan, Cepeda, Pinson, Mota, Cardenas, Perez, Arroyo, Cardenal, Power, Carew. . .

My Cuba has produced its share of great players because of the nation's devotion to sports. In Cuba, baseball is like a plant that is hard to root out, somewhat like "fine grass," a great problem to kill off when it took root in a field of sugar cane. You had to dig deep with your farm implements to weed it out. But it always recurred. Similarly tenacious and indestructible is Cuba's passionate, inborn dedication to baseball.

As a final act to 1951, I was privileged and honored to be named to the American League All Star team by United Press. Joining me in the outfield were Ted Williams and Dom DiMaggio. At first base was Ferris Fain; second base, Gil McDougald; third base, George Kell and shortstop, Phil Rizzuto. The catcher was Yogi Berra and the pitchers, Ned Garver and Allie Reynolds. Pretty heady company for an ex-sugar cane farmer from Cuba to be in.

I felt tremendous. Now, on to '52.

If Minnie Minoso, the fleet, stylish White Sox outfielder, is to be a victim of the second-year jinx which besets so many rookies, there is no evidence of it as the 1952 season moves toward another week.

It may be a bit too early to determine if the new campaign will find Minnie the ball player he was last year, but he hasn't done anything very much different than he did in his first season with the Sox.

Minnie is a never-ending source of fun and amusement to his traveling companions. He is seldom seen without some new article of apparel or a new gadget like a camera, a money-clip or a tie-clasp. Nobody can figure out how he manages to transport all his new hats, shoes, ties, shirts and suits from one stopping-off place to another.

—*Chicago Sun Times, April 23, 1952.*

Top of the 5th

The Sox gave me permission to play only the first three months of winter ball in Cuba because they wanted me to rest one month before reporting to spring training. My countrymen, though, had something special planned for me upon my arrival. There at Jose Marti International Airport to greet me was Cuban President Dr. Carlos Prio Socarras. All of a sudden I was a national hero. A huge crowd was on hand to welcome me home to my native land and I was extremely proud to have made them feel that I brought honor to Cuba with my action on the baseball diamond.

I returned to my Marianao team and during the three months I hit .271. At the end of my contract I spent some time in the country to rest up. I went to El Perico and to the sugar plantations where, as a young man, I cut and harvested the cane. I even brought movies with me and had a film festival with my friends, showing clips of White Sox games with yours truly, naturally enough, in starring roles.

I even took time to work on the farm, loading cane onto the ox-cart. It was a good feeling, working on the farm again, joking with my friends and being with my father. I even told my father to take a vacation for a week while I was there and I'd do the work for him. Many of the workers thought I was crazy, risking injury by doing field work; more so when they saw my shiny new Packard at the edge of the plantation.

I spent two weeks here and another two weeks in Santiago de Cuba, the capital of Oriente Province, where I visited Cuban Mining and the Shrine of Our Lady of Charity in El Cobre. I used to make this pilgimmage annually in fulfillment of a fervant personal vow in thanksgiving to our Holy Patroness for all her protection and for favors she blessed me with.

I saw many old friends, including Senor Sent of Cuban Mining, each and every player on his team, and other people who had helped to make my youth in Oriente pleasant. This was like a mission for me. I wanted to demonstrate to all these wonderful people my desire to share with them the success I had won in the United States as a representative of Cuba and the Cuban people.

I bid good-bye to my friends once again and returned to the Sox spring training camps in Pasadena and El Centro, California. Upon reaching camp, I found that I especially needed to get my arm in shape. It felt weak and I was able to throw only short distances. Two or three weeks were needed for my arm to recover the strength it normally had. As for batting, there was significant change required in timing because the pitchers in the majors throw harder than in Cuba. Consequently, you had to be more alert and ready to adjust to the shorter time allowed you to decide on your swing.

I would also like to emphasize the importance of playing in different ballparks. In Havana, we always played in the same stadium, but not, of course, in the big leagues. Take Comiskey Park, for example. Had I been a power hitter who specialized in long flies rather than line-drives, I would not have enjoyed such success. The fences are too far and often the wind is blowing in. Boston's Fenway Park is difficult for another reason. Often, a new hitter will look at their "Green Monster" of a left field fence, only 315 feet away and think he can easily reach it and smash a homer over it. In reality though, Fenway's distances become much more significant because the Boston pitchers rarely throw a pitch that's high and over the plate. For survival's sake, the overwhelming majority of their pitches tend to be low and on the outside corner. You, therefore, need to expend twice the effort to pull the ball. To be successful, you need to adapt your swing to those pitches by trying to hit to right field. The temptation to go after that "Green Monster" is always there. It has a certain fascination. Hitters persist in trying to clobber a ball over it, and often when a series has concluded and no one has hit a homer there is general remorse. Aside from Comiskey Park, the fields I most enjoyed hitting in were Washington's old Griffith Park, Detroit, Cleveland and Yankee Stadium.

I arrived at spring training full of hope for 1952. We had, in the off-season, acquired the services of three more Cubans, one of whom was the great third-baseman Hector Rodriquez. It appeared our defensive problems at third base were solved. Also joining us were pitcher Luis "Witto" Aloma and infielder Willie Miranda. And we landed another Hispanic, a "go-get-'em" outfielder from Puerto Rico who would soon win the hearts of the Comiskey Park faithful—"Jungle Jim" Rivera. His diving catches and spectacular leaps at the fence gave our outfield a particular flair. With Rivera playing center and me in left, we achieved extraordinary timing and coordination in defense of our assigned territory. We vowed "nothing would get by us" unless it was absolutely out of reach. "Jungle Jim" played out the decade with the Sox and was fortunate enough to participate in the 1959 World Series. Pairing with Jim was one of the more exciting things of being with the "Go-Go Sox." He was a great ballplayer and a good friend.

Believe it or not, I was Hector Rodriguez's interpreter. In fact, he was so dependent on me for communication that some called us "Minoso and his shadow." I knew many comments were made about me and my broken English, but I had purchased a dictionary years earlier and began studying the language myself. When Hector and I became roommates during road trips, we studied together. Many people helped me, but I give special credit for my improvement to Bob Elson. He helped me learn and was a constant source of encouragement.

I avoided learning to swear in English, although I realize these are the words one often first learns when trying to master a new language. Swearing isn't in my Spanish vocabulary either.

When I disagreed with an umpire, I always tried to argue my case in English. Sometimes, though, I ran out of words and continued on in Spanish. Often, if the umpire didn't understand the language he would think I was swearing at him in Spanish. But that wasn't the case. Honest!

I batted well in spring training, despite injuring my hand in the winter leagues. Back in 1952, though, we didn't have the opportunity to play many exhibition games against major league teams because most teams practiced in Florida. Things have changed. Now the Sox hold spring training in Sarasota, Florida. In fact, they have three separate fields, enabling more players to participate in games at any one time. This is a significant improvement, as is "Iron Mike," the pitching machine. At first I didn't like the machine. But I realize now what a valuable asset it is. We are able to speed up batting practice, the arms of the pitching staff aren't strained and the machine throws a greater variety of pitches than do most pitchers, giving the batters a chance to become familiar with all types of deliveries.

I began the 1952 season confident I would pick up where I left off the previous season. I felt that because I hit .326 in 1951, I should hit at least .350 in '52. I was surprised and somewhat upset when I found I was not as productive as in my rookie year. Primarily, it was becoming more difficult for me to hit solidly. My advice to all young players is this: Merely because you had a great rookie season doesn't mean you'll automatically continue your heroic feats. Young players have a lot to prove during their years in the majors and can't afford to become overly confident, assured they have nothing left to prove or learn. A young player should keep in mind that he's been around the league already: the pitchers know what he likes/and doesn't like. Every weakness, every batting flaw he possesses has been documented, analyzed and become common knowledge. Scouts are strategically placed in ballparks, noting how a batter reacts to each type of pitch—curve, slider, fast ball, knuckler... If a rookie shows he's got trouble with any one of them, he's going to become mighty bored in the batter's box, because that's about all he's going to see. If he doesn't learn to adapt, he'll become, as Americans are so fond of saying, a "flash-in-the-pan." Furthermore, outfielders come to know how to play a batter more effectively. They learn where to station themselves in order to be better able to intercept balls before they hit the ground.

The pressure often is overwhelming. When a player sets lofty goals and doesn't achieve them, he tends to push himself. Then things seem to get worse.

All this contributes to the "second year jinx."

In commenting on my problems in 1952, Paul Richards observed in an interview in the *Sun-Times:* "Minnie wasn't getting his base hits, he wasn't stealing bases and, in general, he was not coming up to his talents. Then he began to press. In his eagerness to regain his stride of last year, he was swinging at bad pitches.

"I'm not worried about Minnie because I know he has talent and plenty of it. I know he won't quit on himself. I'm not too much concerned about him because I expect to see him get going almost any day as he did last year. If he doesn't this season, he will next year."

Few things surprised and delighted me more those days than the birth of the *Minnie Minoso-Cuban Comet Fan Club.* Its president was sixteen-year-old White Sox fanatic, Mary Stable. I can assure you she is still a Sox fan because we still keep in touch. I was honored to attend the club's meetings at the YMCA, to answer their questions, give advice and tell them about their favorite subject, the Chicago White Sox. I was always happy when they showed up at Comiskey Park, waving their Club's banner with my name emblazoned across it. I can only hope that, during our meetings, they took my advice to their hearts. I tried to be a positive influence and help set them on the right paths: to graduate from college, have a home and a family.

My relationships with the fans, especially the young people, were more important than contracts and awards. They made the game special. I'm a sentimentalist, and I value most highly the spiritual aspects of life. Among the warmest memories I have of my baseball career is the sincere love and care that was generated between the fans and me.

Unfortunately, 1952 was somewhat of a disappointment, considering our grand expectations after the 1951 season. We finished third, behind the Yankees and Indians, and many of our top players did not match their success of the previous year. Including me. I hit .281, 45 points lower than in 1951. Our leading hitters, Eddie Robinson and Nellie Fox, didn't top the .300 mark, both hitting .296. On the bright side, Billy Pierce, our premier pitcher, had the most wins in the league: 15. I led the league in two categories with twenty-two stolen bases, and my specialty, of course, being hit by pitches.

The 1952 season did contain some unforgettable moments! Specifically, I recall a series with Boston. There was a night game that ran nineteen innings and ended at 3:00 a.m. Not only was that well past my bed time, we also lost. When the affair mercifully ended, I said to myself, "I hope we play twenty-one innings tomorrow." I meant if facetiously, but somebody up there took me seriously, because we almost made it the next day. The game went seventeen innings, but we won, so I didn't feel so tired. In two consecutive games, we played a total of thirty-six innings, the equivalent of four regular games. These were the longest games I played in all my years in the majors, and they had to come back-to-back.

Also, in 1952, I had the honor of being elected by the fans to the American League All-Star Team. I was right behind the great Ted Williams for the left field spot. I was lucky enough to go to the plate once and get a hit, a double. I also scored one run.

The season was over and Hector Rodriquez and I set out for Miami to catch a steamship for Cuba. We drove our own cars and on a stretch of road in Florida, we exceeded the speed limit and were stopped by a state patrol car. We were fined and Hector, always tight with his money, complained it was my fault because I was driving the lead car. I tried to explain to Hector that he was tail-gating me and I hadn't been able to spot the patrol car. Still, Rodriguez never forgave me for the fine and reminds me of it whenever he can. This just goes to show you how grouchy some Cubans can be.

Eventually, we embarked on the *Florida,* with my new Cadillac and Hector's Pontiac on board. It was the first time I made the trip by sea and it was very pleasant. Tourists of that era will recall, I am sure, when trips from the state of Florida to Havana on the *Florida* were memorable what with the music, the dancing, the delicious food and all the entertainment.

I hoped the winter league would sharpen some of those skills which were less than evident during the season. I was looking forward to 1953 and a year which would finally bring my White Sox the recognition they deserved.

Orestes Minoso of the Chicago White Sox was voted Cuba's outstanding professional athlete for 1952 by the Cuban Sports Writers Association.

—United Press, January, 26, 1953.

"Merrylegs Minnie" is what the gals call Saturnino Orestes Arrieta Armas Minoso. They say the way he works his legs as he scrambles around the bases at Comiskey Park reminds them of a sewing machine, stitching steadily away and eating up the yardage. They like the way his uniform fits, the way he smiles and the cute way he always seems to have one pants leg lower than the other.

—Virginia Marmaduke, Chicago Sun Times, June 10, 1953.

Minnie Minoso, fleet outfielder of the Chicago White Sox, suffered a skull fracture as a result of being struck by a pitch thrown by Bob Grim of the New York Yankees last Wednesday, X-rays showed today. Dr. John Claridge, the team physician, said Minoso's temple bone had been fractured. "It's a slight fracture," Dr. Claridge said, "but any fracture is serious. We won't know for several days just how serious this will be."

—United Press, May 24, 1955.

Dr. Harold Voris, a neurologist, tonight examined Minnie Minoso and said there was no brain damage from a small fracture the White Sox outfielder received when hit by a pitched ball last week. Dr. Voris added Minoso might be released from the hospital Friday.

—Associated Press, May 25, 1955.

Bottom of the 5th

My winter season in Cuba was the best I ever played. I hit .327, with thirteen home runs and forty-two runs batted in. I also stole thirteen bases. I returned to spring training full of hope and confidence. As was my custom, I reported a week later than anyone else and some critics thought I was rebelling or holding out. That was pure nonsense and I proceeded immediately to improve my game and my physical condition.

When the season began it was apparent I had left the second year jinx behind and 1953 began to look like an instant replay of my rookie year.

It was my continual desire to give all I had every minute I was on the field. I was anxious to show others I would never let down and was jubilant when I read reports from great baseball men who recognized this all-out approach of mine to the game I loved. Take Leo Durocher, for instance, when he was managing the Giants:

"Give me that guy (Minoso) and I'd really go out on a limb about the pennant race. I think we could win if I had him. He's out there giving you 135 percent all the time. The guy with better talent gives you 80 percent or even less. I'll take the guy like Minoso. Minoso wants to beat you. That's the thing you have to look for, and that's the reason I believe the White Sox have a good chance to win the pennant race."

Or Frank Lane after I rejoined Cleveland in 1957 who told the *Chicago Tribune:* "Minnie is the man who will make the dormant Cleveland fans come to life."

Later, Lane was to say: "To me, Minoso is more than any ball player with the ordinary physical attributes. He brings intangibles to the team that aren't reflected in base hits. His spirit is contagious; it can charge up an entire ball club."

Throughout the year, the battle cry, "Go Minnie, Go," rang in every corner of Comiskey Park. The Go-Go Sox were running a close race with their arch-rivals, the Yankees and the Indians. Cleveland still relied on their Big Four pitchers, while the Yanks had a veteran staff made up of Ed Lopat, Johnny Sain, Vic Raschi and Allie Reynolds, plus a kid by the name of Whitey Ford. Into the fray, the Sox threw Billy Pierce, Virgil Trucks, Harry Dorish, Mike Fornieles and Sandy Consuegra.

There were also some new faces on the roster. We had acquired Ferris Fain from Philadelphia where, in 1952, he led the league with a .327 batting average. Speedster Jim Busby was gone, but in his place was Sam Mele, who proved to be one of the team's leading hitters.

That year was one of my best in the majors. I led the team with a .313 average, slugging fifteen home runs and batting in 104 runs. My attempt at breaking the century mark in RBIs was one of my most memorable moments of the 1953 campaign. We were playing the Indians at home. I already had batted in ninety-eight runs and we were facing Bob Feller. In that game, I connected with one of Feller's patented fast balls and hit the ball over the center field fence. There was a man on and I had my hundred RBIs.

Each coin has two sides, though, and I remember a double header at Municipal Stadium in Cleveland. I had singled against Mike Garcia on a roller that bounced over the shortstop's head. I proceeded to advance to third on a hit and passed ball. We then had men on second and third with only one out, and a 3-2 count on the batter. On the next pitch, I dashed home. I had mistakenly thought we had the bases loaded and there were two out and that no matter what the batter did, it didn't matter if I ran or not. About five feet from the plate I realized my error. The pitch was a ball, the runner trotted to first and catcher asked, "Hey, Minoso, what are you doing here?" I whirled and ran back to third. The throw from the catcher, of course, beat me there and Al Rosen put the tag on me. It was, to put it mildly, a "mental error." When I got back to the dugout, Paul Richards did not put it so nicely. "Minnie," he said, "that mistake just cost you $500." Mortified, I replied, "I deserve a $1,000 fine."

When I arrived at Comiskey Park the following Monday I met Richards. I wanted to give him the $500, but he refused it. "Are you crazy, Minnie?" he said. "How can I fine you? I know you made a mistake, but don't let it happen again. I hope you learned a lesson."

His advice registered. I led the American League that year with twenty-five stolen bases, including three steals of home plate. I might add they were done with precision and my penchant for adding extra bags did not lead to another fine.

At this point, I would like to speak of a dilemma which was on my mind quite often. The year 1953 and those preceding it saw the United States engaged in a war in Korea. Although upon my arrival in the United States in 1945 I had registered with Selective Service, I was never called to active duty. One could say that destiny again had played its magic cards. Yet, if I had been called to serve this country, I would have done so without regrets, in the same manner that I would have fought for my native Cuba. I truly believe that when a country such as the United States is generous enough to offer magnificent opportunities and protection to one who is not a native, this individual should not hesitate to serve when called upon in defense of his country. Although men I idolized—Ted Williams, Joe Di-Maggio, Willie Mays, Hank Aaron and others—had been given this chance, the task was just not in my path. At the time, I often asked, "why not me?" It was a difficult problem to solve within myself, because had I been called, I was willing to go.

Once again, in 1953, it seemed to be open season on Minoso for opposing pitchers. I again led the league with seventeen hits—on me! (My all-time high was 1956 when I was plunked twenty-three times, so I had something to look forward to.) Among my biggest thrills, however, was once again being selected to the American League All-Star Team. I was two for two and batted in a run, our only tally in a 5-1 loss to the National League.

My third season as a White Sox ended with complete reassurance. The "second year Jinx" was a thing of the past and I looked forward to 1954, certainly a year of surprises.

As was my custom, when I returned to Cuba for the winter league, I brought with me supplies of old equipment from the United States—uniforms, bats, gloves, etc. I always left them behind for my Cuban teammates to use when I returned to the White Sox. During the previous year, though, I brought a bat back to the U.S. with me, a Cuban bat, made out of a special Cuban wood called *majagua*. I used it in a game against the Yankees and both the home plate umpire and the pitcher, Eddie Lopat, took an interest in the odd-looking bat (the wood, made from a tree of the linden family, was green). I assured the inquisitive pair that the bat had the correct dimensions and that it was used in the Cuban leagues which, after all, was organized baseball. I further assured them it would not stain the baseballs. So I proceeded to face Lopat and, wouldn't you know it, on his second pitch I swung and broke the bat. Lopat laughed and called in to me, "Keep on bringing those bats from Cuba, those *majaguas,* and I'll keep breaking them."

For the record I usually used a 34$\frac{1}{2}$ ounce bat, only occasionally switching to a lighter one. This was true later in the season when I began becoming tired and weary or when the pitcher was unusually fast and I needed to get the bat around quickly. Later in my career, I preferred a 35 ounce. It was somewhat thicker and I was better able to make contact and produce more homers.

In gloves I preferred using a medium that was perfectly suited to the shape of my hand. It is imperative that a glove be flexible enough so that one can feel the position of the ball. Oftentimes, if a glove is too large, one cannot be certain whether or not the ball is trapped inside.

Upon returning to the U.S. in 1954 for spring training, my destination was Florida, for we had switched to sunny Tampa. We began the 1954 campaign once again with great hopes and expectations for a pennant. I was extremely happy to be a "son of Comiskey Park." Chicago was my home and I thought I would remain there forever. The possibility of a trade never entered my mind. Chicago had, in essence, become another Cuba. I had friends everywhere, especially in Hyde Park where I now resided.

Every game was a new challenge. I felt I had to prove myself over and over again. I responded to "Go, Minnie, Go" with more aggressiveness, enthusiasm and energy. Always, however, I remembered my failings, the errors I made, more than my successes. I felt I owed the fans my very best and that I should get the key hit and make the game-saving catch every chance I got. I also insisted on playing, as they say, "in pain." There were times upon reaching a base that I was in agony because of an injury or a beanball incident.

As I have stated many times, the White Sox fans were always behind me. Sometimes this support was truly welcome for more than just lifting my spirits. Take that time in the 1954 season when I was in the throes of a batting slump—two young ladies from my fan club seldom missed a home game; they even came to batting practice, often bringing a picnic lunch with them. They sat in the stands watching me intently, and it paid off. They told me one day when I was suffering through this slump that I was lifting my left foot when I was about to hit the ball, ala Mel Ott. But I was no Mel Ott and for me to be successful I had to keep the foot flat on the ground. So I concentrated on my foot and was soon out of the slump.

Our 1954 team was power-packed and filled with outstanding hitters. We had Fain, Fox, Rivera and newcomers Phil Cavaretta from the Cubs, Freddie Marsh, Johnny Groth and that great catcher and fine man, Sherman Lollar. We thought our pitching staff, led by Billy Pierce and Virgil Trucks was as good as any in the league. Unfortunately, however, for us and most of the rest of the league, 1954 was the year of the Indians who, with their power hitting and outstanding pitching, set a torrid pace.

The league's headhunters were again zeroing in on me. Once more, I attained the painful distinction of being the leader in HBP, being shelled sixteen times. It puzzled me as to the true cause for these pitches. Were the pitchers trying to scare me off the plate, or did I really crowd the plate? Were these throws truly accidental, or were some of them intentional? I guess I'll never really know for sure.

During 1954, I also suffered a ruptured bursa on my left shoulder, one of the many injuries which were to mark my career. For example, I fractured my skull the following year, managed a broken toe in 1956, had a groin injury in 1957 and, of course, collided with the wall in St. Louis in 1962. This isn't counting the three fractures I received in Cuba and Mexico.

But to get back to being baseball's bullseye, I think any player who's been plunked is looking for "sweet revenge" his next time up. I recall once when we were facing Hal Newhouser in Detroit. He nailed me and in so doing the sunglasses I kept in my pocket were smashed. My next time at bat, I hit a home run. Ahhh, "sweet revenge!"

There were any number of personal thrills for me during the 1954 season. I remember one game in Detroit when we had Ned Garver shut out 2-0 going into the eighth. The Tigers went ahead 3-2 and we were in desperate need of a victory. In the ninth, Eddie Stewart and Nellie Fox got base hits and I came up and lined a homerun to give us a 5-3 victory and enable us to pass the Yankees into second place.

The Washington Senators pitchers were some of my favorite targets during the early going of the season. At one point, I had 29 runs batted in for the year and 16 of them were off Washington pitchers. I even batted in one against the great Bob Porterfield, the only run the Sox had gotten off him all season.

The Indians literally ran away with the flag that year, winning 111 and losing only 43. A new American League record. Still, they couldn't beat the Giants in the World Series when Dusty Rhodes came off the bench to lead the National Leaguers to victory in a surprising four games.

We finished third, with a 94 and 60 record. I batted .320 and posted nineteen homers and 116 runs batted in. In batting, I was only twenty-one points behind A. L. batting champ Bobby Avila of Cleveland. I also had the honor of playing the entire All-Star Game, going two for four.

I can't let the 1954 season pass without telling of one of the most amusing incidents to happen to me in my baseball career. Both the Sox and I were hot during that summer and we were close on the heels of the league-leading Yanks. Stengel wanted to toss a roadblock in our face and decided I was an easy target. So the Yankees called up a fast, quick-handed Cuban infielder by the name of Willie Miranda. Stengel, certain that few umpires and fans understood Spanish, told Willie to hurl epithets at me in our native tongue, certain that I'd be so infuriated I couldn't do my job, especially at the plate. Willie, evidently looking down and seeing the big "NY" on his pin-stripped uniform told Casey "OK." We soon faced the Yankees in New York and Willie dutifully perched himself on the steps of the dugout and began yelling at me in Spanish. Suffice to say old Case couldn't understand the language either. Another thing Stengel didn't know is that Miranda and I were old friends. So Willie hollers out that Case wanted him to shout insults at me and get me so riled up I couldn't see the ball, much less hit it. He asked me to meet him at a local restaurant for dinner. Well, I decided to go for an "Oscar." I stepped out of the box and shook my fist at Miranda and shouted that I understood and I'd see him at dinner.

Stengel was as happy as I'd ever seen him. He complimented Miranda at getting me mad.

Thereupon, I stepped to the plate and smashed a triple to win the game. Casey didn't smile. In fact, he blamed himself for getting me mad enough to do it.

Another incident that makes me laugh today yet is my "discovery" of softball. Warren Brown immortalized it in his column in the spring of 1954. Brown quoted me directly and you'll notice my English was still in its early stages, a way many people remember it to this day. According to Brown, this is how it all happened:

"Other day," Minnie said, "I get excused a little early from practice (this was in Florida). Think maybe I did tell Paul (Richards) I am invite to high school picnic. Anyhow, he let me go early and I go to picnic.

"Do I have fun! The kids play this softball game. They no know who I am. I ask can I get in. They ask I ever play softball. I say 'no, I never do-have.' This is truth. They tell me to play shortstop.

"This game, seems like everyone hit ball in air. I run all over place catching pop flies. Funny thing about that Paul has me, Chico, Cass, everybody practice catching pop flies every day. Paul should see Minnie in this game.

"I catch so many, they want me play someplace else. I say not want play anyplace but shortstop. They ask me again. 'You sure you never play softball before?' I say 'no, I never do-have.' Which is truth.

"After a while I get turn at bat. Do I hit one? Nobody catch that pop fly, I tell you. I hit some more, later on. All left field. Then they all gang up in left and I hit one right field.

"Finally I hit line drive that hits pitcher in the belly. Don't hurt, of course, but I go out to see. He ask me: 'You sure you never play softball before?''

"I say, 'no, I never do-have, but I play a little baseball with hard ball.'

"They tell me I'm sucker to play hard ball when I so good at softball. Somehow they no convince me, so here I am."

The winter season was significant in that I didn't play winter ball in Cuba. Instead, I toured with a black all-star team organized by Dodger catcher Roy Campanella. The squad included such stars as Larry Doby, Luke Easter, Al Smith, Hank Thompson and others. Previously, the black stars had gone to Japan. This year, though, we toured the United States and it proved to be an exhilirating and satisfying experience.

After a short visit with my friends and family in Cuba, I

joined the Sox in Tampa and looked forward to the 1955 season. Never could I have dreamed the kind of year it would be, with the beanball figuring prominently.

During spring training I found myself in the situation of a guinea pig. We were playing the Dodgers and had men on second and third with one out in the eighth. I came to the plate and Dodger Manager Walt Alston ordered the pitcher to give me a pass. That's when the confusion began. It was the first intentional walk to be issued under the new rules which stipulated that the catcher had to remain behind the plate, in his 48 inch box, until the pitcher released the ball. He would then move out to catch the pitch. Charlie Thompson was the Dodger catcher and as the first pitch from Ed Roebuck came in he didn't have to move at all because Roebuck threw it right across the plate. I was on tour and in Cuba during the winter and never heard of the new rule, so I just waited for the pitch to be thrown far outside with the catcher "half-way to first." Therefore, I wasn't ready to swing at it. I was on the second delivery. It was a little outside, but within reach. I tried to poke it to right but missed. Neither pitch had anything on them and I could see that Thompson and Roebuck were beginning to worry. As they explained later, the lines of the catcher's box had been scuffed out and the pitcher had no target. Roebuck said he just lobbed the ball in and was scared I would pounce on it. He also didn't want to throw the ball too far outside for fear it would get away. Thompson knew I could have really pummeled those first two pitches, so he asked Roebuck to put some mustard on the next one and to throw them outside. I eventually got my walk, but after the game I asked my teammates if this was some new National League gimmick. I was told the rule would apply to the American League as well. I vowed then and there to become acquainted with each new ruling handed down.

The season began and again it looked like a dog-fight between the Yanks, Indians and White Sox. Then, on May 18, we were playing in Yankee Stadium in a game which, for the grace of God, could have been my last. I must admit that at times I had trouble seeing pitches in that park, especially on misty days or when white shirts flooded the centerfield bleachers. Hardthrowing Bob Grim was on the mound for the Yankees and one of his fastballs rode up on me. I never believed it was intentional; the pitch just got away from the young right-hander. It hit me in the head and I went down in a heap.

The instant I hit the ground, my good friend and Cuban Heavyweight Champion Nino Valdes, who was in attendance, rushed onto the field and reached my side as I lay at home plate. He was shouting, "That's my brother, that's my brother, leave him alone!" How could anybody have hoped to stop that giant of a man who stood over six feeet and weighted in at 225 pounds? An ambulance rushed me to a New York hospital where x-rays were taken, showing a concussion, but no fracture. I was still dizzy and laid in bed for a few hours. Very shortly, I was visited by Bob Grim and his fiancee. He was truly sorry, so much so he could hardly talk. He began to apologize, but I told him not to worry, that it wasn't his fault.

The next day I flew to Chicago. It was a Monday and a day of rest before we opened against Cleveland. I was met at the airport by my good friend Ernie Carroll and on our way home, I felt like vomiting. I was immediately taken to a hospital where another set of x-rays was taken. This time, they displayed a hairline fracture to the skull. My head was put in a cast and I was placed in intensive care.

I was not allowed visitors for three days, but during that time received more than five hundred cards and letters. Upon my release from intensive care scores of people stopped by to say "hello." Many in the baseball community were concerned that this injury could have an adverse effect on my playing ability.

When I finally returned to active status, the sportswriters and commentators asked me if I were afraid of being beaned again.

My reply, somewhat off the cuff, was, "I don't care if I die!"

They were also curious why I did not change my batting stance, since that was seen as a primary reason for me getting hit so often. "No, I won't change my stance. Yes, I crowd the plate and move into the ball. But I cannot hit any other way. I'm not a wrist hitter. I always see the ball, but I can't always tell which way the pitch is going to break. Grim did not mean to hit me. He visited me many times in the hospital. Nobody, I think, hits me on purpose. When I first came to the big leagues one team always called me names. They would say, 'We're going to hit you in the head, you black ____.' But they didn't mean it. They don't call me names anymore."

After I returned from my convalecence, my bat caught fire. During a two-week stretch in mid-August, I was hitting at a .411 clip and helped the Sox to win ten of thirteen games. Still, it was not enough to win it all, although at the time we climbed to within two percentage points of the first-place Yanks.

It seems there was a side affect to the Grim affair. Upon embarking for Japan for exhibition games with his New York Yankees, Manager Casey Stengel made a rather startling comment on Brooklyn's triumph over his Bronx Bombers in the World Series that fall. "We got licked on the mound, nowhere else, and we were beaten because we failed so miserably in the three games we played in Flatbush. Actually, we lost the series on May 18 when Bob Grim hit Minnie Minoso in the head and fractured his skull. Grim was getting along fine. But that accident ruined his season and lost the series to Brooklyn. Bob became a timid pitcher. From then on he was afraid to skull another batter. He hurt his elbow, got off the active list for more than two months and came back a changed performer. Still, I was confident that Grim would beat the Dodgers. But he just could not forget that beaning mishap and timid pitching could not beat Brooklyn."

The media also concluded that, in addition to using a dangerous stance, I could be a "plate paralytic," or a blind spot victim. They arrived at this belief because of what I said to Grim, that I lost track of the ball that hit me. They also reminded everyone that there was a time in baseball when there were "hit by pitcher" specialists, players who made it a practice to get on base that way and not be injured. It was then up to the umpires to decide if these guys really made an effort to get out of the way of the pitch. The media dredged out such examples as Bucky Harris, Art Fletcher, Frankie Crosetti and Hughey Jennings, the latter setting the all-time record in 1896 when he was hit forty-nine times. According to the annals of baseball lore, the great Cubs first baseman Frank Chance was a hopeless "plate paralytic," getting injured time and again. There was Hall of Fame catcher Mickey Cochrane whose career was shortened after he received multiple shatter-fractures to his skull after a beaning.

I assure you, I wasn't paralyzed at the plate and I didn't have a blind spot. Evidently, I was just an easy target. Paul Richards attempted to clarify this matter in the following way.

"They've hit him a lot at the plate, but I doubt if any of the pitchers are deliberately trying to hurt him or drawing the color line. I would be the first to protest if I thought they were. It's just that Minnie doesn't scare easily. He won't be driven back from his crouch position and he doesn't seem to care whether he's hit or not. There's no type of pitching that bothers him, or if it does, it doesn't bother him for long. He crowds the plate and waits on the ball. He's quick and he has strong wrists. That's why he can wait longer and judge a pitch. And he hits to all fields with equal power. Right now, he's one of the best hitters in the game."

Not only did I ignore the possibilities of intentional dusters, I tended to make light of it when I was hit. During a game in Philadelphia, I was hit in the small of the back. Writhing, I hit the dirt in a cloud of dust, then picked myself up and trotted down to first. On the first pitch to the next batter, I took off like lightning for second and was safe with a stolen base. Again, in Shibe Park, an A's pitcher bounced a fast ball off me— number thirteen of the season. After the game, an air of tension pervaded the clubhouse as my teammates awaited my entrance. I came in grinning. I looked around and could almost cut the tension with a knife. Then I told trainer Mush Esler, "Hey, Doc! You got any white paint? They hit me again. Maybe if I'm white they won't try and kill me so much!"

I never let these incidents get to me too much. There was the time against the Indians when I hit a home run and single off the Tribe's ace Bob Lemon. I decided to visit the Cleveland dressing room after the game and Bob and I exchanged greetings. Then he formed an imaginary pistol with his thumb and forefinger and held it to his temple. Mistaking it for signifying a beanball, I hollered, "Oh, no. I know you guys won't throw at me. You're my friends; we used to be teammates. I expect Philadelphians to maybe try and kill me, but not in Cleveland. You're my friends; we stay that way, huh?" To which Lemon kiddingly replied, "No friend of mine hits me for a home run and a single in one game. I gotta eat, too, you know."

I had to laugh when I read what Casey Stengel told sports writer Edgar Munzel once. To quote Munzel's story:

"One of the fellows who admires his moxie most is Manager Casey Stengel of the Yankees, although ol' Casey gets mighty irritated whenever Minnie gets a free ride to first on being nicked by a pitch.

" 'Why, that guy crouches so far over the plate that you can't throw an inside strike without hitting him,' moaned Casey. 'I tell my fellows to throw 'em inside there with plenty of mustard on the pitch. But that don't scare Minnie. He'll take those fast pitches on the arm or the hip and there he is on first base, getting ready to steal second.'

"Casey's rubbery visage creased into a grin as he admitted, 'It's the sort of thing you like to see on your own club, but you don't want the other guy doing it. You've got to pitch him inside nevertheless. He'll rap that inside pitch down the line a lot of times, but then he's even rougher if you get the ball out over the plate.' "

Good ol' Case.

I had something to prove in 1955—that the beaning didn't bother me. I believe I closed the book on that problem when I hit safely in twenty-three consecutive games in August and early September. My streak was broken by Mickey Mantle when he made a shoe-string catch of a solid line drive. I hit .430 during that streak and raised my overall batting average 39 points.

I played in 139 games during 1955 and went to the plate 517 times. I hit .289, with ten homers and seventy RBIs. I stole nineteen bases and my fielding average was .972. I had only nine errors that year, a significant improvement over my rookie year when I committed twenty-two miscues.

The Sox finished third that year, not far off the lead. We had 91 wins and 63 losses, while the pennant-winning Yanks were

96-58, and second place Cleveland was 93-61. Among the new faces on the team, Walt Dropo hit .280 and George Kell, .312. No contending club had a 20-game winning pitcher. And as far as performance goes, our starters, Dick Donovan (15-9), Billy Pierce (15-10), Virgil Trucks (13-8) and Jack Harshman (11-7) were about even with the Yankees' Whitey Ford, Bob Turley and Tommy Byrne, and the Indians' Bob Lemon, Early Wynn, Herb Score, Mike Garcia and Art Houtteman.

Once again, at season's end, I returned to Cuba. This time I built my dream house, which was located in Havana, in the municipality of Marianao, home of the ball club for which I played throughout my professional days in Cuba. These were very happy days, with my family and friends. My father would visit me often, but he was a man of the country and disliked the city life. He longed for his rural environment and was happier when I drove him back there after playing ball in Cerro Stadium. He resented the remarks many fans yelled at me. He thought they were too critical. He claimed he had to be restrained from striking back. "I will not be back to the ball park," he said. "There are stupid insults against you, my son." I told him it would be wise if he would just listen calmly and try to forgive those who insulted me.

Leaving my new home and father behind, I set out again for spring training once again in Tampa. I was in condition, my injury was behind me, and I was ready to once again join my teammates in chasing the elusive American League pennant.

During training, I began to concentrate more on pulling the ball and on learning to bunt on two strikes, a feat I accomplished often during the regular season. To do this successfully, I would advance against the ball as soon as it left the pitcher's hand. Generally, I would bunt it between first and second, past the pitcher. Sometimes I would hit when the other team expected a bunt. There were times when I would reach first practically walking because the infield was pulled in and there was no one in position to field the ball.

I was now a five-year veteran, and I felt more secure in my position with the Sox. Nonetheless, I still drove for self-improvement. I believe that when an individual ceases to do so, he begins to decline, regardless of his profession. The satisfied, complacent person tends to relax and dwell on past glory. The world of sports would definitely not progress if it were filled with the complacent.

Some things never change, though. In 1956, I established an all-time high of twenty-three hits by pitches, setting a modern American League record. I batted a healthy .316 that year, tops on the club for regulars. Pinch-hit specialist Ron Northey hit .354 in forty-eight times at bat and George Kell batted .313 in eighty trips to the plate. Right behind me were Nellie Fox, with a .296 mark and Sherm Lollar at .293. That year also saw the emergence of a spectacular Venezuelan shortstop wearing a White Sox uniform: Luis Aparicio had replaced Chico Carrasquel at shortstop. He hit .266 in his rookie year, and for the next decade would be one of the finest shortstops in the majors.

Billy Pierce won twenty games that year, but we still finished in third place, this time under new manager Marty Marion. As usual, the Yankees won the pennant. Mickey Mantle won the Triple Crown that year and was voted MVP. My hours spent practicing to pull the ball paid off, for I hit twenty-one home runs that year, a major league high for me.

That pennant was becoming more elusive. Perhaps in 1957...

Minnie Minoso, White Sox, outfielder, Thursday was selected unanimously as winner of the U.S. Ambassador Arthur Gardner Trophy in a poll of Havana sports writers. The trophy is awarded annually to the player in the Cuban League who distinguishes himself in playing ability and sportsmanship. Minoso plays with the Marianao club, league pennant winner.

—Associated Press, Chicago Sun-Times, Feb. 1957.

Minnie Minoso, Cleveland's colorful Cuban who was the Tribe's star of last night's 8-5 victory, almost was forced to sit out the game. He had been suspended and fined $200 by A.L. Prexy Joe Cronin and failed to get up the dough. League office called to remind Minnie to get it up or not play, so he borrowed the money . . . He thought his blast was going to be caught.

—World-Telegram and Sun, July 24, 1959.

"They traded Minnie . . ." The words were said first in shocked disbelief Wednesday night and then in pain and finally in boiling frustration. They were repeated over and over in that emotional sequence wherever an agonized White Sox follower found a fellow sufferer. A Sun-Times survey, undertaken after the receipt of many calls from bitter, protesting fans, confirmed that the news had the impact of a sledge hammer.

—Marvin Quinn, Chicago Sun-Times, December 5, 1957.

Probate Judge Robert J. Dunne opened hearings in a Comiskey family dispute over Chicago White Sox stock today by demanding to know why the Sox traded popular outfielder Minnie Minoso to Cleveland.

—United Press, December 17, 1957.

On the game-winning homer in the nightcap Minnie raced around the bases and ignored all handshakes. "I was having some fun," he explained afterward. It developed he had been fined $200 the day before for not running at top speed on a fly ball to right field which Jim Lemon lost in the sun . . . That's why Minnie dashed around the sacks yesterday. "I show 'em I hustle allatime," he laughed. "I was think maybe I slide into home plate after home run, but I'm afraid umpire throw me out for making too big a joke."

Hal Lebovitz, Cleveland Plain Dealer, June 23, 1958.

Top of the 6th

Every baseball player lives with the knowledge that he could be traded at anytime. Every big leaguer, I think now, but me. I never dreamed the White Sox would swap me. Chicago was my home, my second Cuba. My friends were here; it was the city I loved. But even Orestes Minoso wasn't immune from the realities of baseball and after the 1957 season ended I truly got one of the shocks of my life.

But 1957 was a year I played under a new manager, Al Lopez. The Sox started strong and occupied first place during the spring. The *Baseball Book* of the *Sports Encyclopedia* put it best: "...the White Sox came out of the gate fast. But the Chicago attack, devoid of power and long on singles and stolen bases, could only support their strong pitching well enough to remain on top through June. They proved no match for the Yankees who took fourteen of twenty-two contests from Al Lopez' squad to win their eighth pennant in nine years. The Chicago guerilla attack of Luis Aparicio, Nellie Fox and Minnie Minoso turned out to be no match for the big guns of Mickey Mantle, Yogi Berra and Bill Skowron."

Perhaps one of my biggest thrills that year was the All-Star game played in Busch Stadium in St. Louis. I was sent into the game in the eighth to relieve Ted Williams in left field. In the ninth inning I came to bat with men on first and second and two out with the American League on top 5-2. I laced a hit to right-center off Brooklyn's Clem Labine to drive in a run and make it 6-2. It was to be a most important tally. Billy Pierce was pitching for us and we seemingly had the game in the bag, for Pierce had been virtually untouched in three previous All-Star games.

The Nationals rallied to pull to within two runs in the bottom of the ninth and had men on first and third with one out. Ernie Banks hit a shot to left field off Cleveland's Don Mossi who had replaced Pierce. The man on third scored and Gus Bell, who was on first, raced for third. I knew only a perfect throw would get him. I rifled the ball to Red Sox third baseman Frank Malzone who put the tag on the sliding Cincinnati Redleg. Two out! Bob Grim was brought in to face the next batter, the Dodgers' Gil Hodges.

American League manager Casey Stengel was trying to move me around, but I wanted to stay where I was. I was dancing a tango, up and down in left field, since I insisted on playing short while Casey wanted me deep. Confirming my suspicions, Hodges shot a solid line drive that was dropping quickly. I raced in at full speed and made a shoestring catch for the final out. I kept that ball in my mit all the way to the clubhouse where I had Stengel autograph it for me. I still have it as one of my most precious mementoes. As it so happened, when I was in Mexico many years later, scouts from the United States were showing films of this game in Teohuacan to members of Jalisco's Charros team. There, so many miles and years away, I was able to relive those great moments.

I batted .310 that year with twelve homers and 103 RBIs. I rapped out 176 hits and stole eighteen bases. In addition, I was the league's co-leader in doubles with thirty-six and one of the leaders in slugging percentage with .454. Certainly, I concluded, my spot was secure with the White Sox. I went to Cuba to play winter ball, confident that I would be back in a White Sox uniform the next year and hopefully help them win the pennant.

My Marianao club went all the way that season and represented Cuba in the Caribbean Series, played in Puerto Rico. An altercation arose in one of the games when a line drive got past the right fielder and became entangled in the fence. Confusion ensued. The fans began hurling empty beer cans onto the field and soon the entire diamond glistened from the covering. The game was suspended and resumed the next day. We came back to beat pitcher Juan Pizarro and went on to capture the championship of the Caribbean. It was a great moment for my Marianaos, for Cuba and for me personally.

During the post-game festivities, Antonio Prio Socarras, the Cuban Finance Minister and brother of the President, presented me with a watch bearing an inscription from the President. In making the presentation, the Finance Minister said, "You deserve this token of my appreciation for all you have done for Cuba." I still have that beautiful watch.

The championship was played in early 1958 and, though I was proud and thrilled to be involved in the series, I played with a heavy heart because in December news had come that I was traded by the Sox to the Cleveland Indians. I, along with Fred Hatfield, went to the Indians in exchange for outfielder-third baseman Al Smith and pitcher Early Wynn.

Frank Lane had moved to Cleveland as General Manager and said, though reluctant to part with Smith, believed I'd be an asset to the team. Lane and I had always gotten along fine, though we may have disagreed at times concerning my contract. However, I must admit that I never stayed around long on a team managed by Al Lopez. I found the trade a bitter pill to swallow and although the logic of it may have escaped me for the moment (Smith and Wynn were two of the stars instrumental in helping Chicago win the pennant two years later), I felt hurt and deserted and angry. The special relationship I had built with the wonderful fans of Chicago was torn from me. I couldn't understand why I had to go when my statistics proved I was a team leader.

The trade raised a storm in Cuba and in Chicago. "Bad" and "giveaway" were two of the kinder comments. Even Manager Mike Higgins of the Boston Red Sox said, "Tell them (the White Sox) to keep on trading and they will automatically elevate Boston to second place." In Cleveland, Lane received many favorable letters. He was quoted as saying that he received only two letters critical of the deal.

Later, I learned how the deal was transacted. Lane wanted me, and for more than just my playing ability. The Cleveland franchise was said to be in trouble. Attendance was dwindling and they needed someone to add spark and enthusiasm to the team. Lane saw me as that "someone." As he told Hal Lebovitz of *Sport Magazine* in August, 1958, "I made up my mind to get Minnie the minute I took the Cleveland job. I thought he was the one player in the American League who had the quality that makes fans talk about him when they leave the park. Minoso has that. He did it for us in Chicago. We never drew a million fans until I got Minnie from Cleveland in 1951. That year we drew 1.3 million plus. So long as Minnie played for the Sox, they never drew under a million. So Minnie had to be my man here. When I was in Chicago in 1951, it took me $250 in phone calls and nearly thirty-six consecutive hours on the telephone to get him away from Cleveland. I was prepared to spend at least as much money and energy to get him back again."

The bargaining session took place in December at the major league's winter meetings in Colorado. Lane began talking with Lopez after having had previous conversations with Sox owner Charles Comiskey and Vice-President John Rigney. Lane immediately offered two front-line players, Smith and Wynn. Cleveland wanted another player, but during the course of the negotiations, Lopez refused to part with star pitcher Bob Keegan and said to Lane, "You made the offer. We're not trying to get rid of Minoso. Until you made the proposition, it never entered my mind to give him up."

After the Sox traded Larry Doby to Baltimore, Lane knew they would be more reluctant to give me up. Indians vice-president Nate Dolin then took over at Cleveland's end of the bargaining table. They had breakfast together and Dolin practically begged Lopez to toss in somebody else to help justify the trade if he wasn't going to give up Keegan. So, Lopez gave him a list of four men, and Lane selected Hatfield.

"We regretted to trade Minnie," said Comiskey "but, in return, we feel that in Wynn and Smith, we have strengthened ourselves in two positions while weakening our team in just one spot. We traded Minnie on just one basis, that the players we were getting would help the Sox more this year and over a longer period of time."

I had my regrets, also. I knew I had to adapt to the new situation. Baseball required discipline, obedience and acceptance. I wanted to say goodbye, though, to my friends in Chicago and wrote the following letter to baseball writer Howard Roberts of the *Chicago Daily News*. It was published in the paper in January, 1958:

Dear Friend:

After I had reading all things written about the trade between the White Sox and Cleveland with my person and many other players, I wish to tell something important to the people of all Chicago city.

I don't know why they trade me to another team. It was a surprise for me. Chicago was a great and unforgettable city for me, more than nobody can believe.

For many times, I has thinking that I was born in Chicago, but now the reality my dream becomed fantasy. I has been a lot of fun working with the boys because they love me very much.

If Mr. Comiskey trade me he know why but until this moment I can't find a reasonable motive to do it. Nevertheless, now I am going to another team and even so we are enemys in the games, when I leaving the games I'll be the same friend, the same person.

Cleveland is a good city full of fans who loves baseball very much and I am sure to find in this city the same love for all fans. The must important thing in this moment is to give to the Indians what I gave to Chicago and I am sure to do it with God help and all my own mights.

Good regards for all my friends, member of Minoso's fans club, the press of Chicago city, Mr. Comiskey and the boys of the White Sox. My heart to the people of Chicago city and my special congratulations for the Indians and his fans.

Till we meet again, Sincerely yours,

Orestes Minoso.

As you can see my command of the English language in those days wasn't as strong as it is today. My heart was truly in that letter, though.

I knew there would always be a special place in my heart for Chicago. I recall back in 1955, when I was suffering through a terrible hitting slump and still the fans cheered me, I felt it necessary to make a public apology. I told Dick Hackenberg of the *Sun-Times,* "I no give fans their money's worth this year. People pay to see me hit and when I no hit they got right to say something. But they don't. They very good to me. I apologize to them because I am so bad."

Yes, I truly like the people of Chicago. They made a gentleman out of me. I would miss both them and the White Sox, especially my buddy, Jim Rivera.

Once again, I was an Indian, with the team that had first given me my shot at the big leagues.

For the Indians, however, I began growing a mustache. It was against the rules, but I was holding out for a salary of $45,000 and the mustache was my way of saying, "I'm free." I'm sure Papa Lane did not find it amusing and he approached me to ask what I was up to. I replied that the salary was the same as I would have requested from the Sox. He countered with $40,000 and a Cadillac convertible, but only if I had a good season. I asked him what he meant by a good season. "Hustling," he replied, "always smiling, giving up your free time to kids after the game's over . . . " How could I refuse such an offer. I signed. My first official act as an Indian was to shave my soon-to-be handsome mustache.

The Indians were managed that year by Bobby Bragan, already known in Cuban circles as the manager of the Almendares team. They were again gunning for the American League flag and fielded such stars as Rocky Colavito, Russ Nixon, Mickey Vernon and my fellow-Hispanics Bobby Avila and Vic Power. On the bench were hard-hitting Roger Maris, Preston Ward and my old friend Chico Carrasquel. The Cleveland pitching staff reflected the greatest difference in the teams of the past. Gone were the "big four" of Bob Feller, Mike Garcia, Bob Lemon and, of course, Early Wynn. In their place were Cal McLish, Ray Narleski, Gary Bell and "Mudcat" Grant. We finished fourth that year as the Yankees won once again. And I watched as the White Sox moved ever closer to the elusive pennant—without me.

I hit a solid .301 in 1958, with twenty-four home runs—a record for me—and eighty runs batted in. I stole fourteen bases and, defensively, committed only eight errors in both left field and third base.

Commenting on the deal he had made for me, Frank Lane observed that I had complimented what the Sox had. Lane said I had speed, could throw and was a hustler. He admitted I wasn't a power hitter, but added I wasn't a buttercup hitter cither. The day he said that, I singled against the White Sox, took third on a hit by Rocky Colavito and when our next batter hit a grounder to Ron Jackson at first, I faked a dash home and drew a throw to third. I slid back safely and we had the bases full.

During that season I recall one incident which again proved to me the necessity of being in control of your own destiny. We were in a 0-0 tie with Washington. During my first two times at bat I took the first pitch for a called strike. I was looking for a certain pitch. It occured to me that wasn't too bright if all I was doing was spotting the pitcher a strike, and we were in a scoreless tie. My third time up I decided to hit the first pitch that looked good. The pitcher evidently thought he had an "automatic strike" because he threw a fast ball right down the middle. I swung and put the ball over the fence to give us a 1-0 victory.

Admittedly, my homesickness for Chicago began to fade somewhat because of the warm reception I received from the fans and news media of Cleveland. Once again I wore Number 9 and I freely admit that Ol' Number 9 received great satisfaction whenever *his* Indians beat the White Sox. What's that again about "sweet revenge?"

Adjusting to a new organization wasn't all that traumatic. And why should it be? If one has a healthy attitude, isn't arrogant and is a bit of an extrovert, the move to a new team should go smoothly. One should always know the players throughout the league and to think of the league as a community sharing common interests. When one knows his own limits and respects the feelings and opinions of others, a lasting unity is created among the players. If your baseball career follows this ideal, you will not feel estranged when traded to another team.

One does, of course, have to alter his style of play to conform to his new team's requirements. But this, too, should not present any great obstacles to the professional. One has to learn to work in unison with his teammates, and as the Indians' left fielder, I immediately got my signals straight with the center fielder concerning how to avoid collisions when going after the same ball. Key words shouted between outfielders improve the defensive quality of the whole team. I might add that my style of catching a fly ball, or line drive for that matter, was with both hands upraised. I realize this may differ from many of today's outfielders who seem to prefer catching flies with the gloved hand only. Also, many have tried to imitate Willie Mays' basket catch. But there was only one Willie Mays.

Bobby Bragan encountered difficulties during the season and was replaced in mid-season by Joe Gordon. In one memorable game before the All-Star break we played the White Sox at Comiskey Park. Pierce was pitching and I came to bat with two men aboard. The count ran to three and two and with the next delivery, the runners were going. It was a doubtful pitch, but in a situation such as this, the batter must be 99 percent sure if he lets the pitch go by. I wasn't so positive, so I swung at the ball and foul tipped it. The catcher grabbed it and threw to third for a double play. Glancing at our new manager, I could see he was genuinely displeased.

Unfortunately, I was not selected for the All-Star team that year, so my teammates and I rested in Chicago. Later, on our way to the airport one of them said to me that he thought I was going to be rested for a few days. Joe Gordon evidently thought I was tired. When we opened the second half of the season, I glanced at the first line-up card and, sure enough, my name was missing. So I scribbled over it and later coach Eddie Stanky came over and asked if I had done it. I replied I did and Eddie wanted an explanation. It told him that the manager said that everyone could express his feelings and I was expressing mine. I should be in the starting line-up. Eddie advised that I ease up. This I did, but with great reluctance. I rode the bench for awhile, unhappy every moment. In a game against the Red Sox I was called upon in the fifth inning to pinch hit. On a two and one count, I took a level swing and hit the ball four hundred feet over the left-center field fence. Not staying around for congratulations, I left the park in a hurry. My noisy protest with the bat worked, for the next day I was back in the line-up. But for the first time in the majors, I was the lead-off man.

To say the least I had mixed feelings about batting lead off. Once when I homered, I ran as if the ball were still bouncing around the outfield. The coaches yelled at me to slow down, but I continued to "chase" the other runner around the bases and yelled back that I couldn't because I was the lead-off man.

Also while I was with Cleveland, Manager Gordon tried to alter my batting stance. He thought that if I'd chop at the ball, I'd have greater success. I continually disregarded this advice, and eventually asked him how many Joe Gordons there were, or Ted Williams, or Stan Musials, or Joe DiMaggios. Well, there's only one Minoso and this was his style. I had consistently hit over .300 and didn't see why I should change. I believe managers should not interfere with players whose style of play produces results. They should concentrate on the men who are not delivering and help them improve their performances.

My closest friend on Cleveland was Victor Peyot Power, the great Puerto Rican first baseman. He was a photography buff and very adept at the art. Vic was also somewhat introverted, but once one got to know him, he was a tremendous person.

Bill Veeck and Frank Lane came across with the Cadillac El Dorado at the end of the season and I took the car to Cuba with me during the off-season, along with a Dobermann Pinscher given to me by a family friend. We named the dog Rojo-Ringo and he became our family's escort and watchdog until my father's death.

The 1959 season proved to be one of my most thrilling in baseball, mainly because my Indians fought head-to-head with the White Sox for the pennant.

Surprisingly, there were rumors of a trade, around mid-season, a trade that would have brought me back to the White Sox. I was playing so well, though, that the Indians put a halt to the talks. I was, at the time hitting a respectable .292 and was involved in several decisive games. During a double-header with the Senators, I went seven for eight, including two home runs, one a grand slam.

As I stated, I always desired to beat the White Sox most of all. One vexing moment during 1959 stands out in my mind. During the seventh inning of a tight game between our two clubs, Sherm Lollar hit a deep fly to left. It was about to sail over the fence, but just before it did I ran under it, jumped, hit the fence and caught the ball in the webbing of my glove. Or so I thought. When I came down, an iron bar on the fence struck my elbow, numbing the entire arm. The ball fell out of the glove over the fence for a home run. I went into a rage and began punching the canvas that covered the fence. That homer beat us, 3-2.

Well, the White Sox won the pennant and they clinched the flag in Cleveland. And a few hours later, much to everyone's surprise, the air raid sirens went off in Chicago.

I hit .302 and collected twenty-one homers. I also batted in ninety-two runs. It was a great year for a number of my teammates. Rocky Colavito smashed forty-two homers and the surprising Tito Francona hit .363 and smacked twenty home runs in 122 games. Our pitching was also strong, with McLish leading the way with nineteen wins.

Still, it was the White Sox' year. I was happy for them. But, as every White Sox loyalist knows, their heroes lost to the Los Angeles Dodgers in six games.

The decade had come to an end. I could look back upon some truly productive and memorable years as a big leaguer. My performance steadily improved and now, at age thirty-seven, I was still strong and energetic. The '50s were intense, yet enjoyable. I particularly liked meeting the fans and playing in front of them in the various cities in the league.

Those were also years of learning, of perfecting my techniques at the plate and in the field. I had some tremendous instructors along the way, great baseball men such as Paul Richards, Bucky Harris, Bobby Bragan and my Ambrosia team manager Rene Midenstein who helped me improve as a professional baseball player. I learned to pull the ball to left field more, instead of hitting to right center so often. I developed the art of using my wrists when batting, rather than swinging at the ball without a snap. Armando Marsans was like a professor who opened the minds and hearts of his students, the players. And Adolfo Luque was strict and straightforward. There would never be problems if a player stayed alert and produced effectively. I followed many of his techniques when I managed in Mexico. When Luque reached a decision, it was made to win a game, not to please the public. In this respect, he was very similar to Paul Richards.

Throughout the 1950s, I persistently tried to overcome problems with certain pitches, and during batting practice I'd concentrate on timing and swinging at fast balls. Contrary to some opinion, I feel that the majority of pitches in the majors are fast balls, not curves, because of the problems inherent in throwing the latter. The knuckle ball, of course, gave me the most problem. Just attempt to make contact with one thrown by Hoyt Wilhelm! It's next to impossible! I can't recall what percentage of my hits, doubles, triples, etc., were off of which type of pitch, though I can safely estimate that 50 percent of my home runs were off fast balls.

Obviously, one of the skills I perfected most in this decade was my base-stealing ability. The three base-stealing titles I won in 1951, 1952 and 1953 are among my proudest achievements. Although the strength of my throwing arm in the outfield or at third base didn't improve, I did become faster and more accurate, which are of far greater importance. As the years went by, I depended less on my physical strength, which was decreasing, and more on self-assurance, aggression and knowledge. I never intentionally disobeyed a signal from a manager or coach because the goal of the team was always on my mind and more important than any individual objective.

I do remember once, though, in Cuba when I was playing for Luque. I had reached first base with two out and our clean-up batter up. He had two strikes on him and I reasoned that I should attempt a steal because if I made it I'd be in scoring position and if I didn't, our top hitter would still lead off the next inning. The only problem was that Luque never gave a player the green light to steal on his own. Never! I went down anyway. Ray Noble threw me out with a perfect peg to second. Luque, not known for his even temper, was not the happiest man in Cuba.

When one is a ten-year veteran, baseball assumes the status of a career wherein one has to perform everyday, preciously guard his health and mind and pray his natural faculties do not fail from abuse. In baseball, substitution is a daily fear because no one individual is indispensable, especially a veteran.

Avoiding drug and alcohol abuse is paramount for an athlete, or for anyone else, for that matter. I have seen too many careers cut short because of reliance on them. They are merely crutches which only drives one to lose his self-esteem and the admiration of the fans, managers and fellow-players. I have never grown accustomed to the liberal use of drugs today and I do not accept it. Players who come to the park under the influence of any drug should not be allowed to play.

A sense of pride must always be alive in the minds and souls of players. I was always proud to belong to a first-class team and of being a source of inspiration to my teammates. I was also gratified to be afforded the opportunity to represent the pride and spirit of the Cuban people. Other players, Mays, Musial, Williams, Mantle, Clemente, Aaron and others were driving forces on their respective teams and I was elated to have been placed in their company. A player's attitude, though, must not falter. He must not, as they say, "let success go to his head." To become egotistical is to turn your back on your teammates and on the fans, the people who helped you get where you are.

I was also quite active in civic affairs. I felt it was part of my responsibilities as a professional athlete to visit churches, civic and community clubs, hospitals and institutions for senior citizens, the infirm and crippled children and carry a message of hope, inspiration and faith. I made it my custom to be the first one to arrive and the last to leave. Many times, I imagined I established world records for signing autographs for extended periods of time. I was happy and proud to do this for the public, for after all, look at what the public had done for me. To be perfectly honest, I worried about the day when the fans would forget me and not request my signature any longer.

In my hey-days during the '50s, I appeared on many radio and television shows. I'll never forget the program, "What's My Line?" when I appeared with Nellie Fox. Nellie was disguised as a blonde, and I was made up to look as an Italian. The panelists guessed my identity because of my tennis shoes.

Each American League city I visited with the White Sox had its special charm, a reason that always made me look forward to the trip: New York with its night life of dancing to the many excellent Latin bands; Detroit and visits with my friend Joe Louis; Boston and its Chinese restaurants and sophisticated fans who truly knew and appreciated their baseball; Kansas City and its unparalleled "Kansas City Steak"; Philadelphia, the cradle of American freedom; Cleveland, with its promenades and parks; Baltimore, with its delicious seafood restaurants; St. Louis, with its curious affection for having stop signs seemingly at every corner and Washington,—Washington...a city where great crowds never gathered at the ballpark.

The '50s also introduced air travel. I was, at first, quite leery of planes, especially after jets were introduced. But when our club began using a charter United Airlines DC-6 we became acquainted with the crew.

We only had one close call. On a trip from New York to Boston, an engine caught fire and we had to return to the airport. After a while we learned to accept flying through thunderstorms and heavy winds. With time, I became aware that air travel was safer than any other mode of transportation.

To close out my remembrance of the decade, I think it only right to review what may be my most lasting achievement—getting hit by pitches. My annual totals were: 1951—16, 1952—14, 1953—17, 1954—16, 1955—10, 1956—23, 1957—21, 1958—15 and 1959—17.

I wondered if I'd still be "on target" in the '60s.

I looked forward to another decade in professional baseball, my third. I was being considered an old-timer, but I still felt as enthusiastic and in as good a shape as I did when I was a young man in the sugar cane fields of Cuba, *hoping* some day to be a professional ballplayer.

Marvelous Minnie, brought back to the White Sox after temporary exile with the Indians, again will thrill Chicago. He'll frustrate Frank Lane, the genius who originally brought him to the White Sox and who now is general manager of the competing Cleveland Indians. He'll delight Hank Greenberg, the White Sox executive who, as Cleveland's former general manager, first peddled Minnie to Chicago. And when writers gather to discuss the most entertaining personality in baseball today, I'll say: "Make mine Minoso."

—David Condon, Chicago Tribune, 1960.

Minnie Minoso, usually a very deliberate man around contract time, suddenly turned loose a burst of speed Friday and set the pace in the baseball signing business. Minnie signed his 1961 pact with the White Sox and thereby shattered three records. It was the fastest Minnie ever has agreed to terms (12-minute conference with President Bill Veeck at Comiskey Park); it was the earliest he ever signed, and it was for the biggest salary ever paid by the White Sox. The figure was estimated at $50,000, topping the reported $45,000 received last season by Nellie Fox.

—Chicago Sun-Times, January 28, 1961.

Bottom of the 6th

As things turned out, I missed the World Series by two months. On December 6, 1959, Frank Lane traded me back to the White Sox. Along with me came pitchers Don Ferrarese and Jake Striker and catcher Dick Brown. Sent to Cleveland were catcher John Romano, first baseman Norm Cash and third baseman-outfielder Bubba Phillips.

I quickly signed a contract with White Sox owner Bill Veeck and was thrilled to be once again united with Bill and with the Sox. For the second time, I could be called a Chicagoan. I was just over thirty-seven years of age when I joined the team at their new spring training facility in Sarasota, Florida. It was an impressive gathering, these champions of the American League. Many of them were old friends, some had joined the team since I left, but they were all winners—Roy Sievers, Gene Freese, Ted Kluzewski, Nellie Fox, Luis Aparicio, Al Smith, Sherm Lollar, Sammy Esposito and many others, not the least of whom was my old sidekick "Jungle Jim" Rivera. Al Lopez was still the manager and I must admit I had doubts about whether he would be satisfied with my performance. Fortunately, 1960 proved to be a very productive year. My debut as a Sox returnee could not have been more dramatic had I written the script personally.

It was opening day at Comiskey Park and we were playing

Kansas City. Early Wynn was shooting for his 300th victory and the park was filled almost to capacity.

I went hitless my first two times up and managed a sacrifice fly on my third trip. On my fourth at-bat, I connected for a grand slam home run. The crowd went wild and the ancient walls of Comiskey Park reverberated with the chant of "Go, Minnie, Go." What a beautiful sound to hear. I knew I had not lost the loyalty of the Sox fans.

The game, however, was far from over. Kansas City managed to tie it up. Then, in the top of the seventh, a single was hit to me in left. Two men were aboard and I threw the lead runner out at the plate. The score remained tied and, as fate would have it, another opportunity came my way in the bottom of the ninth. The count was three and one, and I liked the looks of the next pitch. I hit it high and deep to left center and, running to first, watched as it sailed majestically over the fence and into the upper deck. Pandemonium broke loose. The news media reacted as if the Sox had won another pennant.

I was happy to be home!

I played in all 154 regular season games in 1960. This had always been a goal of mine and I had once come within one game. Achieving this objective, however, was not without its obstacles. During a game against the Detroit Tigers, I tried to beat out a grounder and while racing across first base caught my spikes in the bag. I strained a tendon in the leg and was taken off the field in a stretcher. We were playing a double-header and I was advised not to play in the second game. I asked Al Lopez to insert me in the line-up anyway in order to keep my streak going. He finally agreed and the trainer bandaged my leg in much the same manner as Mickey Mantle had his wrapped. In my first at-bat, I doubled to right center, but because I was virtually limping around the bases, Rocky Colavito almost threw me out at second. It wasn't long before Lopez sent in a substitute for me, but I kept my continuous game streak going.

My leg was still bandaged and swollen out of proportion when we flew to Kansas City the next day for a series with the Athletics. There, I visited a doctor who extracted a large measure of coagulated blood from the wounded leg. He ordered me to rest a few days, but I predictably ignored his advice and didn't mention it to the Sox trainer when I returned to the clubhouse. He re-bandaged it and I went on to play.

During batting practice, a woman asked our General Manager for permission to speak to me. Ed told her to go ahead and what she then told me both saddened and inspired me. Her niece was suffering from cancer and she continued in a soft, emotional voice, "Mr. Minoso, you are her favorite player, and I would be grateful if you could dedicate a home run to her." I tried to tell her the best I could that promising a home run was more than I could guarantee, that Lady Luck had to be with a player. Instead, I gave her an autographed baseball and a bat, promising to do my best at the plate that day. Well, let me tell you, Lady Luck is quite a person. I hit a home run over the left field fence and as I circled the bases, practically hopping on my one good leg, I could only think what a lucky guy *I* was. Later, the fan who caught that home run ball brought it over for me to sign. After explaining the situation to him, he was more than happy to trade it for another ball. I signed the home run ball and gave this "special gift" to the woman for her very special little niece.

That particular game was a true slug fest, an unfortunate turn of events for me inasmuch as the merest movement brought pain. Still, I chased down extra base hits all day long, even after my teammates suggested I sit down. I'm one persistent Cuban. Actually, during the 1960 season, I was benched two or three times, but entered the games as a pinch hitter so as to keep my record intact.

The Sox had an excellent year. We ended with an 87-67 record and a team batting average of .270, higher than the Indians (.253) and ten points higher than the Yankees—but the Yankees won the pennant.

Roy Sievers smashed twenty-eight home runs with a batting average of .295. Fox hit .289 and Smith .315. While no single pitcher was a league leader in games won, the victories were spread around quite well with five pitchers winning in double figures—Billy Pierce (14-7), Frank Baumann (13-6), Gerry Staley (13-8), Early Wynn (13-12) and Bob Shaw (13-13). And I'm proud to say that my accomplishments were among the best of my career. I hit .311, while leading the league in total hits with 184. I had twenty homers and 105 RBIs. I stole seventeen bases and made only six errors in the field to win the Golden Glove Award as I had the previous year.

Why couldn't we win it all in 1960? Some people blamed our pitching, but it's hard to say. What one must admit, though, it's that the New York Yankees were an excellent team. They went on to win four more pennants in as many years. When you stop to think of it, the Yankees, and I know die-hard White Sox fans hate to admit it, set a pace I doubt will ever be equalled for endurance. In a space of sixteen years, from 1949 through 1964, they won the American League flag fourteen times. The only teams to interrupt their streak were the '54 Indians and the '59 White Sox, both managed by Al Lopez.

Who can forget the way those Yanks were able to pull their act together, year after year, sometimes after it appeared their magic wand had been broken? This is what *The Sports Encyclopedia* had to say about the 1960 race: "The Yankees began the season unlike a pennant contender, and it seemed as if Casey Stengel's magic was finally gone. After stumbling through May as the White Sox and Orioles led the pack, a repeat of 1959 looked imminent. But the weather warmed, and Stengel got his juggernaut going to make it a three-team race by the time August rolled around. Then, in typical Yankee fashion, they broke the race wide open by winning their last fifteen in a row, a pace too rich for the rookie-laden Orioles and the newly-powerful White Sox...While Roger Maris endorsed Stengel's wizardry by hitting thirty-nine homers and driving in a league-leading 112 runs to be named MVP, Mantle once again provided the super-charge with his league-leading forty home runs. It was a good thing for Yankee power, because Yankee pitching was not the name of the game."

My thoughts of 1960 must not end without mentioning one of my most memorable achievements. It happened in Comiskey Park in a game against Kansas City. I hit a ball high over the left field roof for the longest of my 185 major league home runs. A young fellow outside the park saw it land and brought it to me

for my autograph. According to his testimony, we could estimate that the ball traveled well over 500 feet. The Sox honored
this blast by placing a plaque on one of the park's support
beams which was directly in the path of the shot. Incidently,
there was also a plaque in Havana's Cerro Stadium showing the
landing site of my longest four-bagger there—450 feet.

Being back with the White Sox was invigorating. Hearing the
cheers of the fans in Comiskey Park made me feel as if it were
1951 all over again. I felt young once more. This was my third
decade in the majors and as good as I felt, I never dreamed I'd
only be mid-way through my career as an active big league
player.

However, 1960 was a final chapter in one important way. It
marked the last time I participated in the All-Star Game, in this
instance the last two All-Star Games for these were the years
when two games were scheduled. Unfortunately I went zero for
five in the two contests, but I was honored to be a part of the
American League's 3-M Outfield: Mantle, Maris and Minoso.

The year 1960 also marked the termination of another important element in my life. I participated for the last time in the
Cuban Winter League. The Fidel Castro regime had come to
power and not only were there rumors that amateur baseball
would replace professional baseball in Cuba, there was also
some concern whether the large number of Cuban baseball
players who resided in Cuba but played in the United States
would be able to travel between the island and the U.S. As President of the Cuban Baseball Players Association, I was directly
involved in the situation. I could see there were potential problems, problems of a tremendous magnitude. So you can imag-
ine how bad I felt when I left Cerro Stadium at the end of the
1960-61 Winter Season. I didn't know if I'd ever see the grand
ballpark again.

In addition to me, there were a number of other Cuban
players who would have been affected by "politics." If Castro
disallowed the players to travel or if the United States would
not honor their passports because of diplomatic relations having been severed between Cuba and the U.S., a number of
teams would have lost some outstanding baseball talent. The

Minnesota Twins, formerly the Washington Senators, would have had their pitching staff decimated. Both Camilo Pascual and Pedro Ramos would have been lost to them, as would infielders Julio Valdivielso and Zoilo Versalles. Mike Fornieles would be lost to the Red Sox and Chico Fernandez to the Tigers. Among the other players who would have been affected were Tony Taylor, Pancho Herrera, Julio Bequer, Mike De La Hoz and others. Eventually though, Castro agreed to permit the travel and the U.S. State Department did not bar the way. The Cuban Winter Leagues, however, were a thing of the past.

Upon my arrival in the United States, I settled here, obtaining a permanent residence card and eventual citizenship. My 1961 contract made headlines when the media discovered I was earning $50,000. It was the highest salary ever paid to a White Sox player and Bill Veeck commented, "Minnie is one fellow you don't mind paying well. He gives you more than one hundred percent every minute he's on the field. And, he'd play with a broken leg, if necessary." Although by today's standards this may not seem as much, back in 1961 a $50,000 a year contract was a cause for celebration.

Even so, I thought of myself as somewhat of a transient. Eventually, I wanted to return to Cuba and, although I did invest in some real estate in the U.S., my funds were basically accumulated in Cuba for a future that never came to pass.

Cuba, my beloved Cuba, was now behind me and I concentrated on the forthcoming 1961 season in my new country, the U.S.A.

Minnie Minoso, the ageless outfielder, spoke with drama about his switch from White Sox to Cards. "Perhaps I do not want to move from Chicago," he opened, "but the ball player is like the soldier—orders come, he moves." Minnie is a tremendous favorite among the Cards with his marvelous blend of sentiment, common sense and wit, and he is delighted to be with St. Louis.

—*Joe King, World-Telegram, March 9, 1962.*

The St. Louis Cardinals' outfielder, Minnie Minoso, who suffered a skull fracture when he ran into a wall Friday night, was reported "a little more alert" today, but further examination revealed he also had suffered a fractured wrist. Dr. Stan London reported that Minoso had broken the big bone of his right wrist. The doctor's report said Minoso was "still taking liquids well and was a little more alert than he has been." Minoso was carried from the field on a stretcher and taken to Jewish Hospital, where he was listed in serious condition after the accident. Minoso, thirty-nine years old, will be out of uniform at least four weeks.

—*United Press International, May 14, 1962.*

Top of the 7th

Little can be said of the 1961 season except that it was a disappointment for the White Sox and for me personally. We finished in fourth place with an 86-76 record and my batting average plummeted twenty points below .300. I did hit fourteen home runs and drove in eighty-five runs, but stole only nine bases. The Sox boasted some promising young players that year who produced quite well. Floyd Robinson, for instance, hit .310 and Jim Landis, a fine outfielder, hit .283 with twenty-two homers and eighty-five RBIs. Our top hitters were powerful Roy Sievers (.295 and twenty-seven home runs) and Al Smith (.278 with twenty-eight homers).

There were problems in the air, though. I could sense it and was worried. Bill Veeck was becoming more and more alienated from professional baseball and the possibility of his leaving the game invited a most uncomfortable feeling. Furthermore, the White Sox had a number of veteran ball players, of which I was one. It was no secret that in order to challenge the Yanks, we'd have to mold some young talent and that meant trimming some of the older players. I could only anticipate the worst.

It wasn't long in coming.

I was doing some public relations work for the Sox in November and was in Joliet, Illinois, at a speaking engagement, where I helped demonstrate Iron Mike, the automatic pitching device. Before the banquet that evening, I was listening to the radio and learned the Sox had traded me to the St. Louis Cardinals for first baseman-outfielder Joe Cunningham. I was honestly shattered and felt my heart and soul torn in half.

Depression overwhelmed me at the banquet. All I could think about were the problems I'd face in moving my family, going to a new club and to a new league. I remained calm at the banquet and, as luck would have it, who should I happen to meet there but Joe Cunningham himself. During my speech, I said, "Ladies and gentlemen, when I arrived here to address you, I did so as a member of the Chicago White Sox. However, I am now doing so as a St. Louis Cardinal. I still hope that the Sox win the 1962 American League pennant and that we, the Cardinals, do so in the National League so both teams can meet in the World Series. I wish Cunningham the best of luck in Chicago, as I hope I have good fortune in St. Louis."

The trade was actually consummated on November 27, 1961. My depression did not ease up quickly. For ten days, my telephone remained off the hook; I didn't care to speak to anyone. I even began to think of retirement, but realized I had an obligation to my family, my fans and my career. With a heavy heart I replaced the phone and called the St. Louis Cardinals' general manager.

In January, I attended a testimonial dinner at which awards were presented for the previous season. The Cardinal organization even gave me a tuxedo and two suits with my name embroidered on them. Contract negotiations with the Cardinals, though, were quite lengthy and I returned for a while to do some public relations work in Chicago for a St. Louis-based company. The Cards and I finally agreed upon a contract and I could look forward to attending spring training in about a month at the St. Louis camp in St. Petersburg, Florida.

My wife and I were lodged in a special motel due to the racial discrimination that still prevailed in St. Petersburg. The accommodations were still quite comfortable and St. Petersburg allowed me to engage in some deep-sea fishing during my leisure time. Fishing is one of my favorite hobbies and nothing can compare to fishing in the Gulf of Mexico off Florida's Gold

Coast. I rented a boat for a month and anchored it in front of my hotel in order to avoid a tenseness with whites at other piers. We feasted often on my abundant catches from those clear, blue waters.

I felt good during spring training, despite my wounded pride over being traded. I knew I had a job in front of me, adapting to a new league and its pitching. In an interview with Joe King in the *St. Louis World Telegram* (March 9, 1962), I said: "I know of the players in the National League from the box scores. All players have different ways of doing the job and I must learn the players. They do not know me, either."

In another publication, Oscar Kahan had these kind words: "...the Cuban Comet, aged as he may be, supplies so many 'plus' factors to the picture that the Redbirds outlook has brightened considerably.... Assuming that the Cardinals are able to get that all-around performance, Minoso may be the new element that will provide the crowning touch. The veteran certainly has a history to justify the hope that for one season, at least, he will be able to fill the Cards' long-felt need for a right-handed outfielder who can hit the long ball and drive in runs...Minoso will add another ingredient—color—to a club that often appeared drab on the field. The volatile Cuban should stir up a bit of excitement and perhaps take some of the Cardinals' minds off the *Wall Street Journal* and their outside business investments and interest.... Certainly, he should be a box-office attraction, not only in St. Louis and on his trips back to Chicago, but also in the other National League cities, where fans have heard about him, but have never seen him play."

In an interview with Kahan, I said: "I love the game, I feel like a teenager. Every day, instead of getting older, I feel younger. I'm sentimental. I laugh and I joke. Every team I play with, I make friends. Even if they don't want to smile, I make them smile. But, inside, I'm like a bomb ready to explode. I'm happy to be on the same club with Stan Musial. I hope I can give at least what the other fellow [Cunningham] did. I'm not a home run hitter, but I'm a hard hitter. I can't guarantee anything, but I'll do the best I can for the Cardinals. I've always been proud of my baseball career. The way I feel, I want to play every day.

If they play 300 games, I'll play 300 games. If they play 301, I'll play 301. I am a professional. I wear the uniform I love. We all have to die. What better way to die than in the uniform I love. I'd rather die on the diamond than any place I know. I must be made of iron. Most of the time, after I get hit by a pitched ball and I pick up the ball and I throw it underhand to the pitcher. They get insulted. They say I show them up. But I'm not mad.

"I always have had Number 9 since I've been in the majors, and I made this request of the Cardinals." Ken Retzer who was wearing this number for the Cardinals at the time gave up the number saying that he didn't mind because I ought to help them a lot.

As I began the 1962 season, I didn't know how close I was to come to complying with that statement in the interview about dying in my uniform.

I got off to a slow start, as was my nature. By early May I was hitting a meager .191 and had missed eight games due to a pulled rib muscle. I was, nonetheless, warmly received by the Cardinals fans, who are among the most loyal and astute in baseball. Cardinals Manager Johnny Keane had this to say: "The people of St. Louis have taken him to their hearts. We are very happy with him and we think he is happy to be with us. He had a fine spring and he is giving 100 percent all the time."

Who, though, could have foreseen the unpleasant event that was about to occur?

The date was May 11 and we were hosting the Dodgers in Busch Stadium. The game was knotted at 2-2 in the top of the seventh and the great Duke Snider came to bat as a pinch-hitter with the bases loaded. I was playing him deep in left, but Keane motioned to me to move in. I was reluctant to do so because I had the feeling the Duke was going to hit the ball deep. Still, I followed orders and moved in a few steps. Our pitcher, Ed Bauta, delivered and Snider hit a liner to left-center. It was going over my head and I took off after it at full speed towards the fence. Unaware of having crossed the warning track, I skidded as I experienced difficulty in trying to haul down the drive. I crashed backward against the wall, feeling only the force of the impact. I recall falling, but then lapsed into unconsciousness.

What happened next, I only know from what people tell me or from news reports. I fell on top of the ball and centerfielder Curt Flood retrieved it and threw it back in. I was carried off the field, bleeding and with my face and head beginning to swell. I came to for a few moments and in the dugout and protested that I wanted to keep playing. "No way, maybe tomorrow," was all I heard before once again losing consciousness.

Four days later in Jewish Hospital in St. Louis I finally regained my senses. At my bedside were my wife, Keane, general manager Bing Devine and Bauta, who was serving as translator. They recounted the entire nightmare for me. My teammates and the whole Cardinals organization continued to show extreme concern for me and were most helpful during my lengthy hospital stay, especially the outstanding first baseman Bill White and his wife.

I was also happy and gratified to learn of the concern my old friends with the White Sox were showing.

"Minnie will be alright," assured Luis Aparicio. "So he ran into a wall and hurt himself. I know Minnie, he'll come back and be as good as ever." Coach Tony Cuccinello added, "Minnie will last longer than Satchel Paige, and I think Paige is 75 years old." And my most ardent admirer, Frank Lane, expressed his concern by saying, "I love him as I would my own son. And it will take more than a fractured skull and broken wrist to keep Minnie from playing before too long."

In fact, the attending physicians informed me that the x-rays showed several fractures on the right side of my head near the right ear, plus a fracture under the left eye. My right wrist also received a fracture. Dr. Stan London explained, "Minnie apparently struck the wall with the right part of his head. The x-rays did not show evidence of a fracture Minoso reportedly suffered several years ago when he was struck with a pitched ball."

My remembrance of crashing into that wall are dim. I only recall seeing the ball when it was hit by Snider and I realized I was very near the wall. After that, I draw a blank.

I was released from the hospital a week later and Bill White drove me to my apartment. I was prohibited from driving— doctor's orders. The Cardinals put me on the disabled list for a period of at least six weeks. I must admit, I was deeply concerned whether or not I would ever again be able to play baseball.

The days grew warmer, and one sunny afternoon, I went with some friends to practice on a nearby sandlot. I was only able to bat with one hand. I ran and felt pretty good, but I noticed I was a bit disoriented. I was not lightheaded, but was encountering some difficulty in recognizing people's names and faces. I began to speak less and concentrate more. Slowly, I began to recover.

During visits to the doctor, I was told to close my eyes and walk back and forth. They wanted me to determine the distance between the walls I was told to walk between. After a number of visits, the doctors felt I had recovered sufficiently and authorized me to drive once again. I then let them in on my little secret. I already had been driving for quite awhile.

Minoso is a hard man to keep down!

After the cast had been removed from my wrist, I once again began practicing at Busch Stadium. I needed to regain my abilities in fielding, running and throwing. I toured with the team, but it was not until late in the season that I was able to get back on the roster as an active player. I played in a double-header in Houston and the only mishap was getting hit in the head during batting practice. There were no adverse consequences—I guess my head is used to getting nailed by balls, not walls. The following week I started against the Mets, going two for four, including a home run.

Misfortune seemed to dog me that fateful year. In August, I was hit by a pitch in the forearm. When we returned to St. Louis I asked to be benched for I felt there was a thorn in my bone. During a game in Milwaukee, I was asked to pinch-hit in a tie game with one out and the bases loaded. It was just the type of situation I loved, but had to decline and in perfect honesty admit I was uncertain whether I could do so effectively. My arm was x-rayed and apparently I had a fracture near the wrist I had injured during the May 11 crash. I was forced to sit out the remainder of the 1962 season, a year which, for obvious reasons, occupies a special place in my book of memories.

That year I recorded my lowest percentages ever. Of greatest lament was my batting average—an anemic .196. Despite their great expectations, the Cardinals finished in sixth place with a record of 84-78. The dismal finish notwithstanding, the Cardinals had some excellent players who compiled some truly outstanding statistics. Stan Musial hit .330 with nineteen home runs and Al Smith batted .324 with twenty homers and 102 RBIs. Ken Boyer, Red Schoendienst and Curt Flood also had an outstanding season and our pitching staff of Larry Jackson, Bob Gibson, Ernie Broglio, Ray Washburn and Curt Simmons all posted victories in double figures.

I remained in St. Louis after the season ended. It was a time for retrospection about the May 11 accident and about the various trades I had been involved in. I awaited contract negotiations, for in those days contracts were an annual occurence; players seldom signed multi-year agreements. Admittedly, I thought quite a bit about the trades in which I had been involved: Cleveland to Chicago, Chicago to Cleveland, Cleveland to Chicago, Chicago to St. Louis. They always distressed me, but little did I realize that more awaited me.

It took awhile to adapt to St. Louis. We had initially rented a beautiful house, and later moved to another in a new development. At the time, my wife was expecting a child in June and, to be quite honest, I prayed I would be traded back to the Sox so that our child could be born in my beloved Chicago. Well, as it turned out, our daughter, whom we named Marilyn, wasn't born in a National League city. Instead, she entered this world in an American League city that experienced more than its share of historic turbulance—and tears—in the year 1963: Washington.

But no matter what the future held, I was determined to put the brick wall in Busch Stadium behind me, figuratively speaking, and look forward to a new season, one which, hopefully, would resemble those prior to 1962. I felt healthy and energetic. In the February 2, 1963, issue of *Sporting News,* Neal Russo described the expectations surrounding my comeback to active duty. He suggested that I was the ideal utility outfielder who Johnny Keane was looking for. Russo quotes Keane as saying:

"Minoso is like Stan Musial. They have young bodies, no matter what their age may be. Minnie always has played the full schedule—he average 150-plus games a year for eleven big league seasons up to 1962. He feels fine and I don't see why he can't be counted on."

Keane continued, "Minnie has no pains or after-effects from his injuries and he doesn't put on weight through idleness. At our spring camp, we intend to turn Minoso loose without any restrictions whatsoever. We're not going to ask him to hold back and you know how he has probably more enthusiasm and drive, even today, than anyone on the club." Russo added that "because the Cardinals lost so many one-run decisions in 1962, Keane rates the loss of Minoso among the top reasons for the club's disappointing showing. It was felt that a Minoso performing anywhere like the Minoso of 1961 could have swung ten games from the defeat to the victory column."

Russo quoted me as saying, "I have no effects from those injuries, no dizziness. In fact, I can't even tell where I was hurt. I eat everything, but I'm still 175 or 176 pounds, my playing weight. (I had been working out three days a week at the St. Louis University gym under Cards' trainer Bob Bauman). I feel fine, fine, fine. You know, just a few days after the cast was taken off my wrist, I was lifting heavy trunks and working around my home, and I didn't feel a thing. Minnie will be ready when the door opens in Florida."

There were those, of course, who wondered if I would exercise more caution in the outfield. To these queries, most of them honest and I believe with my safety at heart, my answer was an emphatic "No!" I've hustled all my life and I just can't play any other way. Remember, I was beaned in 1955 and came back strong the following year. Baseball and the United States have been wonderful to me and I'm going to chase hit balls at full speed no matter if there's dynamite under the sod. Every game, every day, is a new thrill for me.

It was now 1963, a year I hoped to prove to the baseball world I could make a successful comeback; 1963, a gut-wrenching, indeed, tear-drenched year for my new homeland, the United States of America.

The magic of Minoso's appeal to the fans is one of the finest phenomena I have ever encountered in sports, yet it is easy to explain because it stems directly from the big heart of this lovable personality.

Dick Hackenberg, Chicago Sun-Times, January 16, 1962.

The Senators made not one move, but two, when they purchased Minnie Minoso from the Cardinals yesterday. The Senators improved the outfield situation and, perhaps more importantly, they added life and pep to a dead ball club. "This is the type player I like," General Manager George Selkirk said by phone last night after arriving at his apartment in Silver Spring. "And I know he's the type the fans will like."

—Merrell Whittlesey, The Washington Evening Star, April 3, 1963.

The Chicago White Sox hired Minnie Minoso as a coach today while Commissioner Ford Frick deliberated over a "faulty rule" under which he vetoed the Sox's purchase of the veteran outfielder from their Indianapolis farm club . . . But today Frick was quoted by Chicago general manager Ed Short as admitting the rule he invoked was at fault and not specific enough for this type of case. "Mr. Frick said he is keeping an open mind on the matter and that a similar case involves the Baltimore Orioles, who want to bring up a player after the Triple A season," said Short. "At any rate, the White Sox think Minoso deserves to be a member of a championship team and we signed him as a fifth coach."

—Associated Press, September 3, 1964.

Bottom of the 7th

I had always been, as stated earlier, a notoriously late starter. I seldom hit well early in the season, but always gained momentum as the year progressed. Perhaps the Cardinals management didn't read my history because they gave me a contract with a substantial cut in it based, not on my overall statistics they said, but because of my poor performance early in the season, before I was injured. Reluctantly, I signed.

Much to the dismay of those who thought I was washed up because of the accident, I was the leading Cardinal hitter in spring training. I knew I was on the road back to a full recovery and looked forward to a second go at the left field wall in Busch Stadium.

Suddenly, I found myself packing my suitcase again, this time en route to our nation's capital. The transaction was completed on April 2, before spring training ended, with the Washington Senators acquiring me for the waiver price of $25,000.

So here I was again, moving on to another city, and making travel arrangements to rejoin the Nats for the remainder of spring training. The word from the Washington camp was that I still had my zip, that I was good for at least another year or two.

I couldn't have agreed more!

I soon paid a visit to my new team's clubhouse. It was one of the most solemn places I've ever been. I said to the men, "Hope things aren't always like this. I hope everybody laughs, 'cause when you're laughing, you're winning."

Speculation on the trade filled the newspapers. Merrel Whittlesey in the *Washington Evening Star* elaborated on this topic on April 3, 1963: "The Senators improved the outfield situation and, perhaps more importantly, they added some life and pep to a dead ball club. Minoso, who has a *Baseball Register* age of 40, is a dashing, reckless veteran, one of the few with a lifetime batting average of over .300. In 1,691 games over 13 years, he's hitting .303."

Another sports writer, Bob Broeg of the *St. Louis Post-Dispatch*, had this to say, "He [Minnie] was fretting on the bench. He wasn't admitting that he had slowed up, and actually he hasn't. Minnie's spirit was still so high he couldn't conceive the Cardinals winning a ball game unless he was in there helping. The Senators got themselves a ballplayer who will do a lot of things, good things, for them."

Even Cardinals manager Johnny Keane told of some reservations about the trade: "My problem with the Cardinals is that I have two outfielders who are set—George Altman and Curt Flood. That leaves me with left field open. I didn't intend to play Minnie too much. After all, I have a man named Stan Musial, remember? Then I have a boy named Charlie James. He's just coming into his own as a ballplayer. I've got to play him or lose him. That left no room for Minnie. I want to tell you there were quite a few in our organization who opposed selling Minnie. He's a popular man and he can still play."

Upon learning of the trade, I told the media that I wasn't bitter, but that I did look forward to playing for the Senators, who, by the way, were one of the new expansion teams. The original Senators of Clark Griffith had moved to Minneapolis-St. Paul and became the Twins. "The Cardinals saved my life," I said. "Nobody was better to Minnie than the Cardinals organization. I'm sorry I was hurt so much and could not help. But, I'm glad to be back in the American League. This is home to me. I don't knock the National League. But it's not the same over there. All my friends are in the American League. I am so happy to be with Mickey Vernon (Senators manager). He is a fine man. When they tell me I am sold to Washington, I am so happy. I am like the first time I put on a big league uniform. I say, 'Minnie, you lucky man. You go to a beautiful place like Washington and you play for beautiful man like Mickey Vernon.' "

During a photo session that followed this press conference, someone accurately observed that it was the old Washington Senators who actually "discovered" me in Cuba. And the man responsible for this discovery was the late "Papa" Joe Cambria, the Nats' ace scout.

Cambria was a fixture in Havana and constantly observed players in Cuban ballparks and in sandlots. His tryouts at Havana's famous Ferroviario Stadium were unforgettable and gave thousands of youngsters and older players the opportunity to become major leaguers. His checkbook was, indeed, part of him and he was ready to sign any good prospects for the Senators' organization.

"Papa" Joe recognized my potential and wanted to sign me *before* the color bar was lifted. I would wish to pay homage to "Papa" Joe Cambria and to other Cuban and American managers and Scouts—Adolfo Luque, Armando Marsans, Mike Gonzalez, Napoleon Reyes, Fermin Guerra, Bobby Bragan and others—for their efforts in giving Cuban baseball players a chance to enter professional baseball in the United States.

Opening day in Washington shall forever be a highlight of my career in baseball. We were playing the first game in Washington's new stadium and the excitement and ceremonies were epitomized by the throwing out of the first ball of 1963. The pitch was made by a man I admired, the President of the United States, John F. Kennedy.

Unfortunately, we lost the game, 3-1, to the Baltimore Orioles and one of the best left-handers in the game, Steve Barber. I went two for four, including a double in the ninth that popped out of the glove of centerfielder Bob Saverine, who had replaced Jackie Brandt. I also snared a line drive, that had base hit written all over it. I was, indeed, glad to be back playing baseball and when the game was over I reveled for a few moments at being a big league regular again. Those few moments, though, were among the most important I ever spent in my life, because they provided just enough time for me to be the last player to leave the field.

I headed down one of the runways under the grandstands that led to the clubhouse. As I looked briefly down another runway I saw President Kennedy. He, too, was leaving the park, but our eyes met and he turned and walked back toward me. He extended his hand and said, "Nice work, Minoso." We chatted briefly and I thanked him for taking the time to come over and talk with me. We all know he was a great sports fan, and he was also a very "human" man for whom my admiration always grew, a man who, in a few months the world would lose. But it was a new season, a new opportunity, and who could have foreseen the horror of Dallas.

Mickey Vernon and I had been teammates before. He was on the Cleveland squad in 1948 when I first became a big leaguer. Our paths crossed again in 1958 when the second Cleveland-Chicago trade brought me back to the Indians. The one-time American League batting champion was one of the finest first-basemen to ever play the game. Vernon was confident I would be the Senators' regular left fielder and that I would play in more than 130 games. Personally, I believed I was still agile and that, playing regularly, I could hit .300.

We began the season terribly, and after forty games our record stood at fourteen wins and twenty-six losses. Poor Mickey Vernon took the brunt of the blame and was replaced by Gil Hodges, another former great first-baseman. Hodges insisted I alternate with left-hand hitting Jim King, meaning I would hit only against left-handed pitching. I was, to put it mildly, upset.

I became depressed because I knew I still had potential and that my batting average sagged because I lacked the opportunity to play regularly. Furthermore, inactivity made it doubtful that I would ever return to my traditional player's form. This depressed me even more.

I don't believe Hodges was right to play me only against southpaw pitchers and I could only conclude that he didn't think I was capable of batting against right-handers. I'm afraid they were hesitant to play me. Evidently, my age and near-fatal accident in St. Louis bothered them more than it did me.

My wife rejoined me soon, and on May 22, our daughter Marilyn was born. Her coming added new purpose to my life and most assuredly aided in my psychological recuperation.

The Senators finished in the cellar that year with an unbelievably bad record of 56-106. It was a poor year for me, too. I played in only 109 games, thanks to the platooning system, and came to the plate a mere 315 times, batting a meager .229.

Few individual good performances could even be pointed to in order to brighten the team's otherwise dismal record. Don Lock slammed twenty-seven homers and Jim King, twenty-four with eighty-two and sixty-two RBI's respectively. I hit but four home runs and drove in only thirty runs. Furthermore, none of our pitchers managed to win even ten games.

The season did produce some highlights, though. And one of the most reassuring, if not vindicating, were the words of Cleveland Indians manager Birdie Tebbets. You will recall, that when I entered the majors I had the ability to hit to all fields. Even though, as they years went by, I learned to pull the ball to left with more regularity, I still hit many pitches to right and center. Tebbetts had this to say: "Nobody took opposite-field hitters seriously at that time (when Minoso broke into baseball). The baseball people thought you had to be a pull hitter. I don't know why, but this ability to hit well to the opposite field seems to be a trait of Cuban and other Latin American ballplayers like Minoso, Cepeda, the Alous and some others. I was with this ballclub (Cleveland) in 1951 when they insisted Minoso change his style and pull the ball. It was between Minoso and "Suitcase" Simpson for one outfield spot. Minnie was getting more than his share of the hits, but a lot of them were to right center, and somebody thought he would hit more home runs if he pulled the ball every time. So they traded Minoso to Chicago and kept Simpson, because he was more of a pull hitter. Simpson had one or two pretty fair years. Minoso, he's still in the line-up. When Minnie showed them he could hit for average and power to all fields, people began taking opposite-field hitters seriously. Then came the Alous and Cepeda."

I am probably as proud of my base-stealing achievements as I am about anything I did in the majors, and this is why June 8, 1963, is such a memorable date in my life. It was a day I attained a milestone. During a game with the Indians, I stole the 200th base of my fourteen year old major league career. I joined three other active players who had reached the 200 mark: Luis Aparicio, 285; Willie Mays, 242 and Maury Wills, 209. Reaching 200 stolen bases had been a coveted goal ever since the introduction of the "lively ball" in the late '20s. I thus became only the twelfth player to attain this figure since Kiki Cuyler did it in 1929. In reading the names of other major leaguers who had stolen 200 bases before me gave me the feeling of truly being in exalted company. There were, for example, Joe Judge and Ben Chapman, and later Pee Wee Reese and Richie Ashburn.

Another personal landmark occurred on July 24 when I batted in my thousandth run. What's more, I got it off of one of baseball's best pitchers, Baltimore's Steve McNally. And I achieved it in grand fashion. The bases were loaded and I came to the plate with 999 RBIs in my pocket. McNally threw one of his famous fast balls and I hit it into the stands for a grand slam home run. When we returned to Washington, James M. Johnston, board chairman of the Senators, presented me with a gold Louisville Slugger bat to commemorate the event. It was a proud moment as my fellow-players, coaches and manager Gil Hodges were on hand to personally congratulate me.

Records and motivation notwithstanding, the Senators released me after the 1963 season ended. It was stipulated, though, that I would work out on a trial basis with the team in spring training the following year. The best I could have hoped for out of this arrangement would have been a utility role at a reduced salary. I remained in Washington that fall and winter, but at last determined not to negotiate a contract with the Senators for the 1964 season.

Then, I was happy to receive a most welcome phone call!

The voice at the other end of the line needed no introduction. My "Papa Number 1," Bill Veeck invited my wife and me to his home in Maryland. I quickly accepted. Thus we spent an enjoyable time in each others' company, with baseball being the primary topic of conversation. Bill invited me to join a tour on an exhibition circuit of Japan. I was ambivalent, for it would mean leaving my wife and new daughter behind. I later regretted somewhat not going, for I missed taking advantage of seeing the Orient.

During our visit, Veeck and I spoke at length about baseball. In the course of our conversation, he asked me whether I would join him if he returned to baseball. I answered that I would go to the ends of the earth for him. Then he asked what I would like to do if I did, indeed, become part of his baseball world once again. It was a pointed question. In that era, there were no black managers or coaches. I looked straight at Bill and told him I'd like to be a coach for him. Veeck told me to come see him if he ever did return to the majors.

During our visit at Bill Veeck's "Castle" I also spoke by telephone with White Sox general manager Ed Short. It was actually a three-way discussion and we decided that I should report to the Sox spring training camp in Sarasota. It would simply be on a try-out basis. There was no commitment.

Upon returning to Washington, I called the Senators office and asked that my gear be gathered together in order for me to pick up on my way to Sarasota that spring. The Senators seemed to prefer that I would be the White Sox's 1964 gamble, not theirs.

During the winter, however, I did have the opportunity to play baseball. I was asked to participate in the Winter League in the Dominican Republic and immediately accepted, for I had seen very little of that beautiful country. There I met my friend Horacio Martinez, who had followed and encouraged my career from Cuba to the Negro Leagues in the U.S. He, in fact, coached the Santo Domingo club for whom I played.

I was a team member for about a month and a half, all the while receiving tremendous warmth and support from the spontaneous Dominican people. We frequently traveled to Venezuela to play games and in turn hosted teams from that baseball-crazy country. During my time in the Dominican League, I had the pleasure of competing with some of the greatest stars in Dominican history: Tony Oliva, the Alou brothers and Juan Marichal, now a member of baseball's Hall of Fame.

I find it hard to express how impressed I was with the Dominican Republic and the 400-year-old capital city of Santo Domingo. Graced by a fabulous cathedral, it boasted many relics of the Spanish conquest.

I felt I had not been playing near my capabilities with the Dominicans and believed it was due to my non-activity with the Senators. I asked that I be taken out of the lineup for I didn't want to hurt the team. The management was astounded, but I insisted, and withdrew from the team.

Although I may not have earned much in that league, upon leaving, I took with me fond memories and unbounded admiration for the Dominican people, their history and traditions.

I wasn't totally prepared for what awaited me in Sarasota. Ten days after arrival for tryouts, Ed Short requested that I pick up my contract. When I did so, I was quite frankly astounded. My salary was $25,000, far below what I had been receiving. Still I signed and, from what I read and was told, was destined to be a reserve outfielder and the club's number one right-handed pinch-hitter.

It was indicated in the press that my duties and potential did not warrant my 1963 salary. Even Senators general manager George Selkirk said his team got me in order to give the Nats a shot in the arm. He admitted it worked. He went on to comment I was a good box office attraction, but I was in a salary bracket the club just couldn't handle in view of the contributions I made. Personally, I considered this an ironic twist seeing as how it was management that was responsible for my idleness, thus bringing about my lack of contribution. I needed to play in order to gain full recovery and I certainly could have performed if I had been in the lineup regularly. They came to conclusions as to how they thought I felt, conclusions which led to my eventual demotion to the minors and my decision to go on to Mexico.

Spring training was always well covered in the Chicago print media. Sportswriter Jerome Holtzman of the *Sun-Times* had this to say: "The irrespressible Minnie Minoso, who had his greatest years on Chicago's South Side, is back with the White Sox and is being given a chance to make the club as a pinch-hitter. After two weeks of spring training, it appeared that Minnie would win a spot on the Sox roster... Always a great hustler and inspirational player, the 41-year-old Minoso hasn't lost any of his enthusiasm. In fact, there are some people in camp who think that Minoso is hustling more than ever before."

Manager Al Lopez agreed: "He still swings with good power. If he keeps looking this good, we'll all be delighted to have him back."

Reading these words, I felt back among friends again, "I'm happy," I replied. "I'm crazy. Like a boy with a new pair of shoes. I feel like a rookie. I must hustle, I must start all over again. But that is fine. That is the way I always am. I always hustle."

Opening day at Comiskey Park on April 14, 1964, was like old times. We had a rookie in the lineup, Don Buford, who had the burden of replacing the great Nellie Fox at second base. But it seems that people thought I carried no pressure. As Holtzman wrote, "Minnie can do no wrong in Chicago."

Still, with all the fanfare, I had a disappointing year. In fact, it was so depressing I nearly quit baseball completely. I appeared in only thirty games, with thirty-one at-bats and a .228 batting average, before the Sox sent me down to their Indianapolis farm club in July. I hadn't seen the minors since San Diego in 1950, and I wasn't happy in the least. It hurt my pride because I still thought I had something to offer as a major leaguer. I even considered leaving the game and joining a partnership in a supermarket chain. But, my burning passion for baseball nonetheless overcame me and I decided to follow my destiny. I reported to Indianapolis.

There, I played third base and left field for a total of fifty-two games. I hit .264, with four homers and twenty-six RBIs. Early in September, the Sox brought me back up—and for the fourth time I "became" a member of the Chicago White Sox. However, I was not re-established in the majors as a player, but as a coach, the first black coach in the White Sox organization. The team was in the thick of the pennant race and they reportedly wanted a "key man." Presumably, that meant me. It was possible that I would also be put on the active list, a prospect which, of course, delighted me. I took batting practice every day, looking forward to the moment when I could step up to the plate and help the Sox win the flag. My return, though, was hampered by legal obstacles. I understood baseball Commissioner Ford Frick invoked a rule forbidding the Sox to sign me as a player. He suggested I might be allowed to play after the close of the Pacific Coast League season September 13. But my comeback was not to be, and that September I was left with an empty wish.

The White Sox finished one game behind the pennant-winning Yankees that year. Many credit their near championship to the fine pitching by the "big three": Gary Peters (20-8), Juan Pizarro (19-9) and Joel Horlen (13-9). The all-round quality of the staff enabled the Sox to make such a spirited run for the pennant. The team appeared to lack consistent hard hitting, though. Floyd Robinson did bat .301 and Pete Ward was the top slugger—.282, twenty-three homers and ninety-four RBIs.

Many were convinced I could remain a permanent coach with the Sox. A position would be open for the following season and, although I was physically conditioned to resume playing, I had no objection to coaching.

Fifteen days after the season ended, I was handed my unconditional release. It was a shattering blow to my aspirations and my self-esteem. I found it hard to comprehend my days as a major leaguer were at an end, that nobody wanted me any longer. I really thought that, although forty-two years old, I was gaining new impetus. Apparently, I was alone in this belief. I had to face the facts, and the facts were quite clear. I was being set aside and far as I was concerned, headed toward oblivion.

After some thought, and some soul-searching, I came to the conclusion that I wasn't through and can look back on the year 1964 now as the year of dramatic change. I determined to set out in search of new challenges in another land which seemed to welcome me.

My years as a big leaguer were behind me now, and as I left Chicago for a new career in the game I loved the cheers of the wonderful fans in Comiskey Park echoed in my ears. I could close my eyes and still see that fleet-footed young Cuban circling the bases to the chants of "Go, Minnie, Go!" No matter where I may be, I know that somewhere in the heart of Minnie Minoso, it will always be 1951.

Now it is the same thing all over again. All that has changed is the names of the towns because now Minnie is a member of the Charros de Jalisco team in the Mexican League. "I went down to Mexico," he said, "because I wanted to find out for myself...if I can do these things without hurting myself... without getting on the rubbing table every day. I went to see Veeck last year before I went to Mexico. Veeck said to me: 'Minnie, you've still got a year or two to play. Why not try to hook on?' I said to him: 'Veeck, I'm just like you. I believe I die before I go down on my knees to beg. I have pride... perhaps it is too much pride...but that is the way I am.'"

—*Tom Fitzpatrick, The Chicago Daily News, Feb. 11, 1966.*

Anybody familiar with Minnie at all won't even by overly shocked by the disclosure he's tearing it up for the Culiacan Tomato Pickers in Mexico's Sonora-Sinaloa winter league or that he ripped a pair of line drive base hits in his last two times at bat against Mazatlan the other night.

—*United Press International, December 21, 1969.*

Would you believe, Minnie led the Sonora-Sinaloa Winter League in batting with .359? He played at first base and in the outfield. He may be 47, but he's 25 physically. Anyway, the Mexican League the Triple A summer circuit is expanding and Minnie is going to manage one of the new teams, the Durango Union Laguna. He's going to work closely with the Orioles, keeping us abreast of the young talent in that league.

—*Frank Lane, 1970*

Top of the 8th

Baseball was thriving in Mexico. Minor league franchises had already been awarded to Mexican cities and both winter and summer leagues had for many years been fully operational. The opportunity to participate presented itself, and I debated whether to go "south of the border" to play baseball.

I could have stayed in the United States as a public relations man for a midwestern company. It had one chilly drawback, however. I would have had to do extensive traveling to as far as Denver on roads which, during the winter months, were often snow-packed and icy. I also considered joining the supermarket venture mentioned earlier, or even establish my own business in Chicago.

None of these possibilities, though, could have compared to the lure of baseball. It was in my blood. Alvaro Lebrija, owner of the Charros de Jalisco and general manager Jesus Carmona had little trouble convincing me to join their Triple A team. It proved to be a big move on my part for I remained a member of their organization for most of my eleven seasons in Mexico. In negotiating with them on the phone, I said I would sign on one condition—that if I did not feel my usual love for baseball or be able to give 100 percent all the time, I wanted them to release me with no recriminations.

It was agreed and I began making arrangements to move my

family from our temporary hotel room at 68th and Stoney Island to more comfortable quarters. Orestes, Jr., however would stay behind when my wife and daughter eventually joined me in Mexico.

My son, incidentally, had received quite a write-up in the local press. It forecast that he would be the next Minoso in the majors. Although only eleven at the time, it was reported that he was on the threshold of a brilliant baseball career. He was also called "Minnie" and was batting .370 in an Evanston, Illinois, Little League. The story complimented me by stating he looks, acts and plays baseball like his father. It credited my son with being responsible for his team's first-place standing. Orestes, Jr., did, in fact, receive his first glove when he was two years old and was playing in the Midget League in Cuba when he was six. He also played Little League in Long Island and St. Louis.

His Little League coach in Evanston, Bob Cullen, said, "He's just a natural-born athlete. The ball never gets by him in the outfield. He's right on top of it at the crack of the bat."

Proud of him as I was, I could only say: "As long as he's a good team man and alway tries to do better tomorrow, that's what counts. I don't really care if he plays baseball. The main thing is school. I want him to be a good citizen."

After resettling my wife and daughter, I left for sunny Mexico in late 1964 in a raging blizzard. Driving was extremely difficult, but I arrived in Laredo, Texas, without incident. There, I began the process of clearing my car through customs and establishing my visa. All this took a few days, even though a call to the Charros' management in Guadalajara cut through most of the red tape. This was to be my first lengthy stay in Mexico, although I had visited the border towns of Nogales and Tijuana when I played for San Diego and trained with the Indians.

I signed a contract for $10,000 plus bonus for the 1965 summer season. I wanted to meet with immediate success in Mexico, and I recalled years before telling Alejandro Pasquel, the Mexican baseball impressario who tried to sign me to play in Mexico instead of in the American Negro League, that if, indeed, I ever did play in his country I would give it my all. Although Pasquel had been killed earlier in a plane crash, my words still held true.

I apparently have a knack for breaking in with a team in a big way. My debut in Mexico was extraordinary. I came to bat as a pinch hitter in a tie game with the bases loaded. The first pitch from the southpaw was a knuckle ball for a strike. The second pitch was a carbon copy of the first. I swung and drove a single to left which won the game for the Charros. The next day I also was fortunate to come to bat as a pinch-hitter with the bases loaded. Again, I singled to win the game. From then on, I was a regular.

Throughout the 134-game season, I battled for the batting title with Poza Roca's powerful Emilio Sosa. I finished five percentage points behind him when the season ended, 365-360. I had 169 hits in that 1965 season, with fourteen homers and eighty-two runs batted in. I played left field and third base (just like in the old days) and made only eleven errors. I considered my return as a regular a great success.

My league, the Mexican League was composed of eight teams and performed during the summer months, April through August. The Mexican Pacific League, also classified as Triple A, played its schedule during the winter months. In addition, there were a number of other leagues throughout the country. Comparing the two Triple A leagues, I always considered the Pacific League as the stronger because its winter schedule allowed its teams to field players from the majors in the United States.

I had little trouble adapting to Mexican baseball and my statistics bear me out. The fans even called me, "The Charro Negro," the black cowboy. One must admit that Mexican fans are somewhat more passionate about the sport than are fans in the United States. They were known for making rude remarks in the stadium, yet I know they didn't really mean them. Outside the park they were delightful.

The Charros represented the entire state of Jalisco, though our home stadium was in the historic and beautiful capital city of Guadalajara. We competed throughout Mexico and I had the pleasure of playing with and against scores of truly first-rate athletes, many of whom later made it to the majors.

I must admit to one other favorable experience of my days in Mexico. I was once again able to express myself in my native tongue. Although I gradually gained competence in the English language, I was always, and I think you'll agree understandably, more comfortable conversing in Spanish. I realize the press had some fun with me in my early days in the majors about the way I murdered the English language. But my dictionary and Anglo friends helped me over many rough spots and, although I admit I'll never be a scholar in my adopted tongue, I rather doubt if very many of those who good-naturedly laughed at my vocabulary could have survived for long in Latin America without an interpreter.

By returning to active duty, I was certain I had recaptured the abilities I had for awhile forfeited in St. Louis. I regained a sense of fulfillment and a knowledge that I was truly needed. I was filled with a new set of ambitions for, quite frankly, my performance as a rookie in Mexico was very similar to the one that made headlines in Chicago during the 1950s.

Soon my family joined me and we moved into an apartment in the Lupe Building. Eventually, we obtained a hacienda that was to be our home for the next eleven years. We thoroughly enjoyed our stay in Guadalajara and its surroundings. Its year-round moderately warm climate results in some of the most ideal weather in Mexico.

We travelled extensively that first year, not only in association with my playing schedule, but because we wanted to enjoy as much of this beautiful country as possible.

Both my achievements on the diamond and my travels with my family were more than satisfactory that year, and I quickly settled my 1966 contract with little difficulty.

Again, during 1966, I competed for the batting crown; this time with the great Hector Espino, nicknamed the "Grenadier of Chihuahua." And again, I finished second, this time with an average of .348. Throughout most of the season I was hindered by a fractured finger caused by—you guessed it—a pitched ball. I hit with the finger taped, a condition which caused considerable discomfort whenever I swung the bat and especially when I made contact with the ball.

Before the injury was even known, though, I gave injections to the broken finger prior to game time in order to numb the pain. The Mexican League season is divided into two rounds and I was advised near the end of the first half to have my finger operated on. Well, I agreed to this, but, out of superstition, postponed the date originally scheduled because it was the anniversary of the day the great bull-fighter La Russo was killed.

Eventually, the operation was performed and I was ordered to rest for ten days. Naturally, I didn't heed the order and went on to play. While batting against the famous Silverio Perez, I found I was unable to swing the bat. I returned to the clinic where the physicians found traces of chipped bone in the injured finger. Another operation ended the problem.

Although my Charros were unable to win the pennant, I was content with my life in Mexico. My confidence grew. In addition to my .348 batting average in 1966, I recorded 131 hits and forty-five RBI's, with seventy runs scored. I played a new position—first base—and my nineteen errors attested to my unfamiliarity with it.

Still, somewhere within my subconscious, the White Sox remained. The Comiskey Park telephone number often flashed before my eyes and I had visions of the Sox calling me or I calling them. It was but a dream, of course, a wistfulness for the past. Those days were gone forever.

During 1966, I was interviewed by *Chicago Sun-Times* columnist Tom Fitzpatrick. His words, in an article that year were quite poignant and I would like to share some quotes with you here:

"Life has come full circle for Orestes (Minnie) Minoso. Minnie, who captured the hearts of American League fans during the fourteen seasons he spent in the majors, is back making the long overnight bus trips from one minor league town to another. When he broke in with the New York Cubans of the Negro League more than twenty years ago, Minnie grew used to sleeping in a sitting position while the bus droned 200 or 300 miles to the next town.

"Now it is the same thing all over again. All that has changed is the names of the towns...."

I explained to Fitz why I wanted to play in Mexico.

"This is the one profession that God gave to me. I'm going to do it until he tells me that I can't do it anymore or shows me that I can't.

"I went down to Mexico because I wanted to find out for myself...if I can do these things without hurting myself...without getting on the rubbing table every day."

I told him of the respect I had for the fans in Chicago and how I would not want to make them ashamed of me because of the way I played. I also told Fitz why I wouldn't try to "hook on" with another team, in other words go to a team's camp without a contract. It was the same answer I gave to Bill Veeck a short while before when he posed the identical question to me. I said to him:

"Veeck. I'm just like you. I believe I die before I go down on my knees to beg. I have pride...perhaps it is too much pride...but that is the way I am."

Fitzpatrick finished his story with these very warm, mellow words: "Minnie stopped talking. He stared straight ahead through shining eyes and swallowed hard several times in the silence that suddenly settled over the tiny room."

The Winter League of 1966–1967 produced another famous first for me—I became a player/manager for the Orizaba team of the Mexican Pacific League. This league had some unique rules. For example; restrictions were imposed concerning the number of foreign players allowed on each team: three was the maximum. At each game, the managers had to carry their payrolls with them so that the league officers and umpires could verify the total paid to the nine in the field did not exceed the allowed quota, taking into account both the domestic and foreign players. If an excess in the payroll was discovered, the club could be fined or the game forfeited. So intricate was the system, that the players themselves did not understand why they were benched during certain games. To my recollection, the maximum payroll allowed for each team in each game was between 150,000 and 200,000 pesos.

I never found managing and playing a burden. To confirm

my own feelings, I always thought of Lou Boudreau with the Cleveland Indians. He was both a great manager and an outstanding (Hall of Fame) player. I was afforded the opportunity to manage because the league really needed to develop professional baseball talent and needed my experience as a big leaguer. Then, the Mexican Leagues were in their budding stages. Today, they are vast reservoirs of major league prospects. A most recent "graduate" is Fernando Valenzuela, the pitching phenomenon of the Los Angeles Dodgers, who came from the Pacific League.

The techniques I followed in managing, I owed to my Chicago White Sox mentor Paul Richards. It was a technique built on mutual respect between manager, coaches and players. I encouraged everyone to think they were members of a large family. I insisted on frank and open communication and treated each player as an individual, without any show of favoritism. Discipline was, of course, essential, but if a player missed a sign I refrained from reprimanding, and hence embarrassing, him in public. Rather, we would discuss the matter in private. Ideally, we should avoid tenseness at the ballpark and strive for teamwork at all times. Unity and camaraderie are the keys to success. Of utmost importance, management must understand that the players are human beings with feelings that need to be respected.

In managing a team, it became quite apparent that, although the squad may look great on paper and have some "big names" in the lineup, the performance may not be a winning one. Statistics are what count, not names. Managers cannot perform miracles and a player should not use his field boss as a scapegoat for a poor season.

I was responsible for my own decisions. I disliked pressure from others, whether it was from players or management. As manager, I exercised the sovereignty which I felt should go with the job and rebelled against orders from above. This explains why I only managed that team for one year. We were losing, and losing by big scores. Pressure from management soon prompted my resignation. As a player with Orizaba, I played in thirty-six games and hit .350, including five homers, and played both third base and the outfield. The team, however, finished in seventh place with a dismal 40-66 record.

Obviously, my first try at managing was not a resounding success. Still, I aspired to eventually manage in the United States, be it in the major or minors. I felt I was well-qualified and experienced in the game. After all, some major league managers did not even play in the big leagues, or if they did, were up for a very short time.

I played only thirteen games with the Charros in 1967 and hit a less than spectacular .243. I remember, though, that when we traveled to the El Bajio territory we often played against the team managed by the father of former White Sox star Jorge Orta.

I toured a great deal in the southeast area of Mexico during that time, visiting the Yucatan, Tabasco and Quintana Roo. Here, the fantastic Mayan ruins dominate the landscape. I enjoyed walking midst these centuries-old remnants of a by-gone culture representing a people whose achievements in the arts, sciences and architecture marvel researchers today.

I also managed in 1968, this time the Puerto Mexico team of the Southeast League. Our home base was Coatzacoalcos. The team, a farm club of the Charros, had abundant talent, including pitcher Maximino Leon who later went on to play for the Atlanta Braves. I also inserted myself in the lineup a number of times in order to help inspire the players.

The Puerto Mexico fans were a very special breed. The city had been without baseball for about twenty years and they truly wanted a championship. They were extremely displeased at my frequent commute to Guadalajara, wishing I would remain with the team for longer periods of time. In fact, every time I returned from Guadalajara I was greeted at the airport and the stadium by mariachis. Attendance was fantastic at every game with 12,000 fans filling the stadium to capacity. I believe we gave them their money's worth, finishing in third place with a 57-36 mark. Personally, I was more than satisfied with my performance. I batted .366 in fifty-six games, getting fifty-three hits and socking four home runs.

With our parent club in Guadalajara, I played in twenty-two games, compiling a batting average of .296 and performing flawlessly in the outfield and at first base.

I was a busy man that year because I also served as a designated hitter for the Venados team of Mazatlan in the Pacific League. I hit over .300 and was even involved in the play-off. And, that same year I served as player/manager for the Union Laguna club in the Bajio League, whose members included many Charros. It was quite an experience. In addition to playing and managing, I was also assigned to oversee the construction of the club's new ballpark. I helped measure the field and contracted to have it cleared and bleachers installed.

The following year, 1969, I resumed my dual role as player and manager with Puerto Mexico. We did not fare as well as the previous year and finished fourth, with a 56-59 record. I played in seventy-four games, much to the delight of the ever-enthusiastic fans, and hit .301. With the Charros that year I hit .320 in thirty-six games. All the while, I was gaining a reputation as a person knowledgeable in the game and I was gratified to know others considered me, "the old man," an inspiration to others. This confidence was expressed in 1970 when the Charros annointed me as an emissary to revive baseball in the town of Gomez Palacio. It amounted to an entirely new commitment, almost as if I had been traded, for I remained there for the next four years.

There hadn't been a team in Gomez Palacio for sixteen years. The last person to attempt the revival was Cuban Hall of Famer Martin Dihigo. Well, a team was put together in 1970 and I again acted as player/manager. Gomez Palacio was, indeed, "hungry" for baseball and an aura of excitement prevailed as we opened the season. The relatively small stadium seemed inadequate to hold the cheering throngs wanting to see their new team in action. As a player I alternated at first base with Idelfonso Ruiz, an outstanding player. Once again, I paid homage to my tradition and hit a home run in one of the first games of the season.

I took up residence in Gomez Palacio, renting a room in a small hotel. Gomez Palacio was one of six teams in the league.

The others were: Saltillo, Chihuahua, Juarez, Sabina and Monterrey. Each of these teams had a number of excellent players; fleet, slick-fielding Zoilo Versalles, for example, was in our league for awhile. Also, many talented young players developed their abilities here and later played in the United States.

I managed Gomez Palacio for four years, applying the Paul Richards formula of personalized attention and team spirit. We finished third in 1970 and fourth in 1971, while I batted .468 and .315 respectively.

It was true, that during my years in Mexico I was removed from the hectic pace of the major leagues. Still, I was pleased to know that my career was nonetheless being followed in the U.S. For example, on December 21, 1969, a report filed by UPI stated: "Minnie Minoso is still playing ball. That in itself isn't mind-bending news or, particularly, is the fact he will be forty-eight his next birthday. Anybody familiar with Minnie at all won't even be overly shocked by the disclosure he's tearing it up for the Culiacan Tomato Pickers in Mexico's Sonora-Sinaloa Winter League."

Moreover, according to Frank Lane, who observed me in Mexico, "He played first base and in the outfield. He may be forty-seven, but he's twenty-five physically."

I couldn't stay away from Chicago for too long a time and returned in the summer of 1971 to play in an old-timers game prior to a Sox double-header with the Washington Senators. Sportswriter Wendell Smith of the *Sun-Times* had this to say about my return in his column of July 27, 1971: "Saturnino Orestes Arrieta (Minnie) Minoso returned to town Sunday for the Old-Timers game at Sox park and was the same as when he left six years ago, trim, affable and bubbling over with baseball enthusiasm.

"He still injects Spanish into his delightful conversation when at a loss for English words, which means you have to be alert and listen carefully when he speaks because, otherwise, you find yourself utterly confused with his dual version of your native language.

"Ever since he reluctantly shed his White Sox uniform, Minnie Minoso has continued to play baseball. Playing daily in

Mexico has enabled him to retain his youthful appearance and zest for the game. He looks no older than when he joined the Sox as an outfielder in 1951. And, according to those who have seen him in Mexico, still plays the game with the same wild abandon that he did in Chicago for nine exciting seasons."

Further in the column, Smith relates the conversation I had with Senators' manager Ted Williams when I visited the Washington clubhouse prior to game time. Williams told of the time in Boston when I tried to run on his throwing arm which he admits was not the strongest in the league. I had lined a hit to left-center, good for at least two bases. Williams ran over, picked it up and reared back to throw. I rounded second and made as if I was going to third base, in order to draw the throw and a possible error. I took a few quick strides, then put on the brakes and wheeled to return to second as I was sure the ball was coming into third. The second baseman was waiting for me, with the ball in his glove, and tagged me out. Williams had thrown the ball behind me. I'm still not sure if Williams outsmarted me or I outsmarted myself. In any case, I was one very embarrassed and unhappy Cuban.

My years in Mexico continued to provide undeniable evidence of my ability to play baseball regularly, and play it well. In 1972 with Gomez Palacio, I hit .285, with twelve home runs and sixty-three RBIs. And in 1973, I managed a .265 mark, again with twelve homers and eighty-three RBIs.

I left the Charros organization after the 1973 season and most of my last two years in Mexico, 1974 and 1975, were spent with the team in picturesque Puerto Vallarta, a mere four hours drive from Guadalajara. I played first base and in my first year with the team we won the pennant. True, it may have been only a five-team league, but it was still a thrill to win the pennant— any pennant.

In the play-off series against the Diablos Rojos of Mexico City, I again was lucky enough to play an instrumental role. It was a best of seven series and we were leading three games to two when I was fortunate enough to hit a home run in game number six to win the championship. During the awards ceremony, I was paraded around the stadium on my teammates' shoulders. I was even requested to make a speech. It was a magnificent experience to be a winner. Perhaps we were only the team from little Puerto Vallarta, but I guarantee you the Dodgers couldn't have felt more jubilant had they beaten the Yankees.

As a matter of fact, the Puerto Vallarta team won three consecutive pennants. And each time, the town feasted and celebrated for three days with outdoor dancing, eating and drinking. I doubt if this record was ever equalled, or approached for that matter, by any American or National League city. As a side note, because of our success, the stadium had to be enlarged in order to accommodate the cheering throngs.

I also played in the little mining town of Cananea. I was also the team's coach and batting instructor, not to mention managing the team for some time. I mention my brief stay in Cananea for a very special reason: my son, Orestes, Jr., played on this team.

Our Cananea team was quite good and we were in the thick of the fight for the pennant. Our primary opposition was Agua Prieta, a town located about fifty kilometers away. They had beaten us in the previous meeting and we were now due to play them in the decisive series of the year. But in order to qualify for the playoffs, we had to win eight of the remaining nine games. Quite a challenge, but one I was confident our team could meet.

I believe part of their dedication to winning was the result of my demands as a manager. For one thing, I emphasized punctuality, both for games and practice. And drinking prior to playing was totally banned. There was no resting during practice and if I saw a player leaning against the fence or otherwise "dogging it," I would soon *persuade* him to get busy. Also, because so many of these players were local boys, I prohibited excessive talking to friends and relations during practice. Proper guidance and discipline were important and I encouraged them to trust me as a leader, not as a dictator. Above all, professional behavior was imperative.

We went on to win the eight games we needed and entered the play-offs against Puerto Penasco in their own ballpark. They were leading 3-0 in the seventh inning of the decisive game. We scored two runs in that inning and had the bases loaded when I sent myself into pinch hit against a left-hander. They had just changed pitchers and couldn't do so again until I finished my time at bat. "Old Minnie" must have looked too formidable because he walked me to tie the game. Then they brought in Enrique Romo, who hurled for the Pittsburgh Pirates, to pitch to the next batter. Romo lost his control, tossed a wild pitch, a run scored and we were up 4-3. In the bottom of the eighth, they also loaded the bases with one out. I immediately changed pitchers, bringing in our ace Guzman to face their slugger Estrellita Ponce. Guzman went on to strike out both Ponce and the next batter and we held on in the ninth to preserve our victory and the championship.

Victories in Mexico are always headline-making events. Following our win, a great fiesta ensued. We were met sixty kilometers outside of Cananea by hundreds of cars and a multitude of cheering fans. This happy caravan escorted us into the city, picking up scores of others fans and vehicles along the way.

Our entry into town resembled that of a victorious army, or at the very least the traditional entry of the gladiators. Each member of the team was interviewed on the local radio station and we all sang, as a chorus, a tune a hometown composer had arranged for the glorious occasion. Really! The fiesta lasted three days and the streets were filled with singing, dancing, eating, drinking and rejoicing citizens. We were heroes!

The Charros, meanwhile, had signed Orestes, Jr. He had earlier forfeited his major league career after spending time in the Kansas City organization.

I was soon offered a chance to coach for the Hermosillo team in the Pacific League, but turned it down because I felt myself more qualified to be a manager. Eventually, I was given the position of managing the Leon team of the Mexican League.

With them, my years in Mexico were coming to an end. Looking back, I can truthfully say I emerged as a capable leader. I gained a reputation of being able to handle various types of players and to demonstrate a multi-faceted capacity in the sport. These were exciting years in Mexico and I enjoyed a wonderful time in a most hospitable and colorful country.

As a player and manager, and as a scout for Bill Veeck, primarily to keep him abreast of prospects in the Mexican leagues,

I travelled the length and breadth of the nation. I enjoyed its many attractions and closely observed the countryside, cities, towns and people. All showed a common denominator: hospitality and joy. My wife and daughter joined me on many of these travels. I would now like to relate to you some of my observations of numerous Mexican attractions. Each of these places occupies a special place in my heart and in my soul. I only wish each of you could have the opportunity to enjoy them as I did.

Let us begin with Monterrey, Mexico's industrial capital.

Beer and steel have uniquely combined to put this city, at the base of 5,700-foot Cerro de la Silla (Saddle Mountain) on the map. The steel mill is the largest in Mexico and the beer of the Cuauhtemoc Brewery is the finest you'll find anywhere in the world. Textiles, furniture and chemicals are also produced here and the famous Kristelurus hand-cut crystal is an exclusive product of the town.

Tradition and history are important elements of life throughout Mexico. In the pleasant little city of Merida, for instance, which arose from an ancient Mayan city, the descendants of the founding family still live in the house built by their ancestors in 1543.

Morelia is another town where history is of paramount importance. Its architectural designs are maintained to resemble those of old Spain and it is a city famous for its woodcarving, pottery and copper.

Queretaro is just the opposite. Built around the production of opal mines, it is a city of the future with many new industrial enterprises constantly locating here.

I found Zacatecas, in northeastern Mexico, to be one of the most enjoyable of my adventures in Mexico. Named after an Indian tribe that inhabited the area at the time the city was founded, Zacatecas is known primarily for its gold and silver mining, and for its vast mineral baths. When the Spaniards settled the town centuries ago, most of the income from the mines was returned to Spain. What little remained was used to build the cathedrals and palaces that fill the city.

Guadalajara, my "hometown" during most of my stay in Mexico, occupies a special place in my heart. This city, the capital of the state of Jalisco and second largest city in the country, saw its greatest growth during the 1920s when the Southern Pacific Railroad extended its tracks from California to Jalisco in order to open new trade routes.

It is a city of plazas and parks that provided me with many hours of quiet contemplation while I was a member of the Charros. The center of Guadalajara is dominated by its magnificent cathedral, dating back to 1571, from which four plazas extend in the form of a cross. Each of these plazas is in a way unique unto itself and during the summer all of them are alive with the color of flowers and trees to give everything in sight a festive and joyful appearance. The cathedral, though, is what the visitor always remembers. It took a half century to complete and incorporates a half dozen architectural styles, including Gothic, Tuscan, Moorish, Mudejar and Corinthian. And when its 200-foot high towers were toppled by an earthquake, they were rebuilt in Byzantine. In all, there are eleven altars and in the sacristy is a masterpiece by the great Spanish artist Murillo. Many of the art treasures were sent by grateful King Ferdinand in appreciation for funds the city donated to Spain during the Napoleonic Wars.

The government Palace, built in 1643, contains the greatest historical interest in Guadalajara. It is here where Mexico's greatest president, Benito Juarez, escaped execution in 1858 during the War of Reform and where Father Hidalgo declared the end of slavery.

Almost the direct opposite of historic, traditional Guadalajara is modern, thriving Acapulco, Mexico's tourist mecca. It started out as only a small fishing village, but grew after World War II to become one of the hemisphere's leading vacation lands.

Acapulco is best known for its beautiful sandy-white beaches and warm blue waters. Caleta, the best known beach of the west coast, is especially nice for its placid waters. On the other hand, Condesa, on the east side, is the place to go for those who like the rougher surf. This is the "in" beach which comes alive with music and dance in the early afternoon and has open beach restaurants of all kinds to whet your appetite.

Then there is the "city of tiles," colonial Puebla, fourth largest city in Mexico and so named because the four extinct volcanoes near the city have made the area rich in the material needed for making tiles.

Puebla is the most characteristically Spanish of all major cities in Mexico and its architecture is typically colonial. I travelled to this beautiful city often and was always impressed with what has become known as the Secret Convent of Santa Monica. In 1857, church reform laws abolished convents. Santa Monica, however, was secretly operated until its discovery in 1935. It is now one of the world's foremost museums of religious art, containing thirty-nine rooms filled with paintings and relics from this and other secret convents.

Puerto Vallarta, where I played baseball for two years is, I think, one of Mexico's most picturesque and interesting cities. It is the only colonial port city in the land and located on Playa del Sol or Sun Beach. Originally it was called Los Muertos, or Deadman's Beach, so named because centuries ago, pirates would leave their dead on the shores. Its name was changed, for reasons that would seem obvious, to attract tourists. Located south of the city is the popular beach of Mismaloya. Often did I relax on this beach, to enjoy the welcome rays of the sun and the cool breeze off the deep blue waters.

Of special interest to movie buffs is that Mismaloya was the scene for the filming of "Night of the Iguana" and for many years Richard Burton and Elizabeth Taylor maintained a mansion here. Movie director John Huston still has a beautiful home here and is one of Puerto Vallarta's most honored residents.

Any visit to Mexico would, of course, be incomplete without time spent in the capital of Mexico City, the site of the original Halls of Montezuma. It was the ancient capital of the Aztec Empire and today the entire area boasts temples, palaces and pyramids built by these first citizens of Mexico. The attractions here are legion and every time the opportunity presented itself I did not hesitate to visit this, one of the most outstanding cities of the "New World."

The National Palace, for example, stands on the ruins of an Aztec Temple. Its foundations were ordered built by Hernan Cortez. This structure houses the offices of the President of the Republic and of special interest is the bell which hangs over the central tower. It is the same bell which was rung by Father Hidalgo in the city of Guanajuato to signal the start of Mexico's War of Independence.

The Mexico City Cathedral is the largest in Latin America. The magnificent church was begun in the year 1567 and completed 250 years later. It contains religious artifacts dating back hundreds of years.

None of my many visits to Mexico City would have been complete without a leisurely stroll through beautiful Chapultepec Park, 2100 acres of greenery, fields, gardens, playgrounds and lakes. It even contains a small zoo. Situated smack in the middle of Mexico City, it is a haven from the hectic pace of the capital, a place to reflect and to enjoy the beauties of nature.

Chapultepec Park epitomizes what I had come to know during my many years in this country—that no matter how busy or harried you may be, you'll always find a spot of beauty, a place for quiet contemplation.

Before I relate to you my return to the United States, I wish to tell of a very special chapter in my life: the time I managed a team with my son, Orestes Jr., on the roster. The team was Cananea and I was proud to be able to be the senior partner of a father and son team. But as you will see, all was not ideal, for it is not easy to be both a strict disciplinarian field general who cannot show favoritism and a proud father at the same time.

To begin with, Orestes Jr., arrived in Mexico after having played in the outfield of Class A and Double A teams in the Kansas City organization. I often wondered whether, if I had been in the United States when he entered organized baseball, my son might have joined the White Sox. Unfortunately, it is a question which shall remain eternally unanswered. He encountered problems in the minors and eventually came to Mexico and joined the Leon team and later my Cananeas. While playing with Cananea, Orestes Jr. established an all-time record of hitting five grand-slam home runs in two months. That's quite an accomplishment in any league.

As I watched him play, I knew he had great potential for the majors. His throwing arm and fielding ability were probably better than mine had been. Luck, however, was not on his side and the right opportunity never presented itself. My son played in Mexico for a time, then left baseball altogether to devote himself to working with the Jehovah Witness Organization. As his father, I am proud he selected a righteous, clean and decent way of life through a commitment that has brought him personal satisfaction.

I would want to state here how happy I was to manage a team on which my son played. Orestes Jr. was a fine player and a gentleman. Proud as I was, though, it wasn't the easiest task in my life. I continually had to be on guard against charges of favoritism. Often I was reminded of movies where a commanding officer's son joins his unit and the officer goes to great lengths to demonstrate he is just another trooper, sometimes making it even rougher on him. There were times I had to apply this ramrod straight "John Wayne" requirement on Orestes Jr.

For example, we had a player on the team who continually missed signs. He missed a bunt signal in a game we were losing 5-2 and I subsequently removed him from the game. A couple innings later, my son came to bat. I flashed the bunt sign to him because we had a man on first. Instead of bunting, he swung away and hit into an easy double play. Orestes seldom missed a sign or disobeyed them. At the end of the inning, he started walking up the steps of the dugout to go back on the field. I ordered him to stay where he was.

"You missed the sign," I said to him. "You sit on the bench the rest of the game."

Orestes became very upset. He believed I was trying to show him up in front of the fans, but I would not hear of it. I told him to be quiet, that I was the boss.

We lost the game. Afterwards, some fans approached the dugout and found me alone, crying. They said I was his father and that I was too tough on him. They insisted I should not have taken him out of the game. I tried telling them how difficult it is to have your son play for you. I'm not sure if they understood.

To me, a baseball team is one big family. One cannot show favoritism to anyone. Not to your brother. Not to your son. I would not hurt my son. But, by the same token, I would not have been a good manager if I did not respond to him in the same manner as I did to others.

At age fifty-three, Minnie Minoso believes he is being reborn in this Bicentennial year. After an absence of thirteen years from the major league baseball scene, he has returned to one of his top stomping grounds, Comiskey Park. Thanks to a call from his old friend Bill Veeck, who gave him his big league chance, Minnie is now stationed at first base, coaching for the White Sox. "I'm very happy to be back in baseball," said Minoso from his hotel room in Milwaukee Wednesday. "I grew up in it. Now, it is like life starting over again. I think I can help any organization and I have a good opportunity to improve myself. This is like a school for me. I never thought I could make it back to the big leagues. I don't know if I will be with the White Sox for the rest of my life. I like to think I could manage in the minors or maybe even the White Sox someday."

—Dennis Lustig, The Cleveland Plain Dealer, June 12, 1976.

Players in batting slumps often make adjustments in their stances to break the bonds that bind them. Minnie Minoso, 0-for-3, Saturday in his dramatic return as an active White Sox player at age fifty-three, opened his stance for Sunday's first game of a doubleheader. He hoped to prevent overstriding. It worked. Minoso slashed a fastball by young California left-hander Sid Monge into left field on the first pitch in his first at-bat. He thus became the oldest man ever to hit safely in the major leagues. Satchel Paige and Nick Altrock performed when they were fifty-nine and fifty-seven, but they were pitchers.

—Joe Goddard, Chicago Sun-Times, September 13, 1976

Bottom of the 8th

In the mid-'70s, my future and the future of the Chicago White Sox seemed to hinge on one man, an innovative showman with a peg leg, a man whose entire life read like a box score, the man who has been one of my closest and dearest friends: Bill Veeck.

Bill bought the White Sox in 1975, partly to save it from a possible move out of Chicago. As usual, he was determined to build a winner and a hustling team that would bring the fans back through the turnstyles.

I had always kept alive the hope that someday I would return to the majors, preferably with the White Sox. As the years went by, that hope was admittedly beginning to fade.

It was the fall of 1975 and I was in Puerto Vallarta when the phone call came for me. It was Roland Hemond, the general manager of the White Sox. He said Veeck had been trying to reach me for three days. Hemond then spoke the words that made my heart skip a beat. Veeck wanted me to rejoin the team as a coach. I was elated. I was on my way back to the majors and to the White Sox, working for not one of the baseball men I most admired, but two of them, for Paul Richards was to be the field manager in 1976. I wanted to shout my good fortune to the world. Unfortunately, Hemond told me I was to keep news of my return a secret for a month.

A secret?

It seems Bill Veeck, never at a loss for grabbing a headline, was going to announce my hiring at a banquet being thrown by the Chicago baseball writers who were honoring Bill with the Comeback Award. It was in honor of Veeck buying the Sox and rescuing them from a possible sale to outside interests and a move to another city. An honor to be sure, but Bill couldn't let it go at that. He didn't want his image tarnished, so he decided to do something special. I was his *special*! Not only would he announce my return to the White Sox, he would present me in person. I was to be his "mystery man," as he told the press, and the sportswriters were left to speculate just who this "mystery man" was. Naturally, Veeck got more coverage than would normally have been the case.

Doesn't he always?

So I agreed to keep it a secret. I did tell my son, and we embraced and cried happily. According to Orestes, Jr., who told the press later: "It was early in the morning when the phone rang. Dad answered and I half heard what was going on. When dad came back, he opened his arms and told me he was going back to the White Sox. We embraced. It was a moment I'll never forget. He said he'd be wearing Number 9 again and that he'd be going back to the city he loved and to the people who loved him."

It was, indeed, a great break for me. How I wanted to share the news with everyone. Twice Paul Richards called to congratulate me.

The big event took place in January, 1976, and I arrived at O'Hare Airport the day of the banquet. I was met by my good and faithful friend Ernie Carroll. From that moment on, I lived incognito. Ernie whisked me away to the Palmer House Hotel in Chicago's Loop where I was told to remain in my room and not to talk to anyone, especially on the phone. Shortly before the banquet began, Minnie the "mystery man" was escorted downstairs to the Grand Ballroom of the Palmer House where the big event was being held. Chicago sports fans had wondered who the man of mystery was for about a month now and an

overflow crowd of a thousand at this posh soiree would be the
first to find out.

The grand moment had arrived. But I'll let Jerome Holtzman's story in the *Sun-Times* the following day describe what
happened next:

"There was much guessing and some of the guessers did hit
upon Minoso, but they were guesses, nonetheless, because
no one let the cat out of the bag, so to speak. Hence, it
wasn't until 9:50PM, January 11, in the final hour of the
scribes' dinner, that there was no need for any more guessing. It was at this moment that Veeck told the crowd: 'The
fellow who is really entitled to this award (the one presented to Veeck) is a gentleman by the name of Orestes
Minoso.' Then, from the back of the Grand Ballroom entered Minoso, escorted by Ernie Carroll, his long-time
friend. The crowd gave Minoso a three-minute standing
ovation. When Minnie reached the podium, Veeck presented him with the William Wrigley, Jr., Memorial Award
for *Comeback of the Year,* an award that had been given
to Veeck minutes before. It was a poignant and memorable
moment, one to be treasured in Chicago baseball history."

I was moved, and with understandable emotion, I spoke to
the gathering, thanking them for their salute to me and expressing my gratitude to Bill for the award and for giving me the
chance to, once more, be a big leaguer.

Predictions were rife as to how I would be used by the Sox, if
not exclusively as a coach. Designated hitter was often agreed
upon. Veeck, however, said, "I don't know about that. We'll
have to see how things go in spring training." But, there was no
doubt I would be a coach, probably at first base. Paul Richards
was, in fact, starting with two coaches who had played for him
more than twenty years ago in Chicago. I, of course, was one
and the other was Jim Busby, the fleet-footed center fielder who
was at the heart of the "go-go" spirit when it began. Tragically,
our great second baseman Nellie Fox was struck down by cancer a short while before. Had he lived, it was said that he, too,
would have been asked to return as a coach. Veeck also insisted

that my return was considerably more than an attempt at nostalgia. "He's always been a fine baseball man," Veeck said. "Anyway, this is where he belongs."

Two or three days after my "re-appearance" at the Palmer House, I returned to Puerto Vallarta, expecting to join the Sox later at their Sarasota, Florida spring training base. In Puerto Vallarta and the adjoining town of Tecuala, the newspapers published reports of my return to the majors. The natives jokingly referred to me as a "Gringoide," one who had deserted the Mexican Leagues and returned to the U.S. Yet, they all shared in my happiness. I completed the season with Puerto Vallarta Club and Veeck and I began to make final arrangements for my eventual arrival in Sarasota. I was informed that I was already part of the Sox payroll.

Farewell parties in Mexico abounded after I officially terminated my affiliation with the Mexican League. I bid good-bye to my friends and fellow players. There were hugs and there were tears, but most of all there were smiles and well-wishes, for we were all happy I was once again a member of the Chicago White Sox. Finally, my Cadillac and I were on the road— destination: Chicago. First on my agenda was arranging for living quarters for my wife and daughter. Then I was occupied with a variety of speaking engagements. I remember one presentation especially. I wore a new pair of patent leather shoes and they were too tight, causing great discomfort. When I returned to the hotel, I immersed my feet in hot water. That was a mistake. It only caused my feet to swell, thereby aggravating the situation.

The next day, Mr. Hemond and I boarded a flight for Sarasota and the Sox spring training camp. My feet, however, were killing me, so I took off my shoes. Everyone laughed. "Just like the good old days," I said, "during my childhood in the sugar cane fields of Cuba." That incident and my shoeless entrance into training camp in Sarasota will never be forgotten. I wonder how many people recall another White Sox player who long ago became known for lack of shoes. What true White Sox fan would not call to mind the great and tragic "Shoeless Joe"

Jackson. Anyway, Veeck ordered an electric vehicle for us to use while we toured the training site and inspected the diamonds. When my feet finally got back to normal, I began formal training.

I was once again associated with the great Paul Richards and as a coach, I was able to view baseball from another angle, gathering more experience and insight. Because I was close to him on this level, I was to learn a great deal. A big league coach is obliged to put forth added effort in order to assist his manager in carrying out orders and plans. A coach has to be alert at all times to assure that players do not relax and that they exert themselves to the maximum. Players must be in peak physical condition. Those in need of additional batting and fielding practice must receive it and the coach must note who is in need of additional drilling.

My assignment was to coach the first base line. From this position I would pass along bunting and hit-and-run signs. I was also required to give batting tips to the hitters. A coach must have responsibility, authority and a decision-making capacity in order that he may perform to his optimum ability. I felt very satisfied and proud at being able to handle the task of coach with a self-confident feeling of leadership.

The entire coaching staff was a harmonious group. We understood and respected each other and the players. We did, indeed, have many good young players, just as we did twenty-five years earlier when I first joined the Sox. Only now their names read Lemon, Bannister, Barrios. . . . We were trying to plant the seeds of excellence now which we were confident would germinate in the future. Regarding his coaching staff, though, Richards insisted we assume responsibility and make our own decisions. . . and to always remember that the good of the team came first.

Granted, the fans may not always agree with the decisions we make, but we must all, the manager especially, stand our ground. We are the people truly aware of how a player is functioning. From the dugout, we are able to determine the opposing team's strategy. I was able to incorporate Richards' methods with my own experience to analyze and thoroughly understand the art of playing and managing a team.

One is continually learning in baseball, and with experience we can be right most of the time in our decision-making. But we all need a certain technique, and Paul Richards had one all his own. As I said, he never showed favoritism and he tried to understand and appreciate everyone as equals, dealing with each individual according to his personality. His positive attitude affected everyone. He held his temper in check, unlike some managers, and although he rarely smiled and was firm, he demonstrated great respect towards everyone.   .

Opening day at Comiskey Park in the Bicentennial year of 1976 was unforgettable...another one of those career highlights which made me feel I was a very lucky man. I must admit my heart fluttered as the starting lineups were being read over the P.A. A new major league season was about to begin and I felt a special tug at the heart when the names of the manager and coaching staff were announced. What happened next, I couldn't possibly have anticipated. The moment my name was announced, the more than 40,000 fans in the packed stadium rose and cheered as one. The applause lasted for a full five minutes. I was dazed and I saluted the fans by doffing my cap and throwing them kisses. I couldn't believe, that after so many years in Mexico, I was still remembered with such affection in Chicago.

In the bottom of the first inning, when I went to my position in the coach's box at first base I reflected on my years of association with Chicago—the comings and goings, the years of triumph and the days of farewells. I had been the first black to break the racial barrier in the city and I must admit some regret at not being given a coaching position earlier. I could even have served as a designated hitter since I had many productive years ahead of me. Indeed, circumstances made my years in Mexico the only viable alternative. I can't help but think that if Bill Veeck had been with the Sox in 1964, he would have made it unnecessary for me to begin my career anew in Mexico. In truth, I always admired the way the crosstown Cubs handled their great star Ernie Banks after his playing days were over. Ernie was always a member of the Cubs organization.

But this was 1976, and another beginning. Dennis Lustig, in the June 12 *Cleveland Plain Dealer* observed: "At age fifty-three, Minnie Minoso believes he is being reborn in the Bicentennial year. After an absence of thirteen years in the Mexican League baseball scene, he has returned..."

Lustig went on to say how happy I was to be back in Chicago and to be starting over. I went on to tell him, "I don't know if I will be with the White Sox for the rest of my life. I like to think I could manage in the minors or maybe even the White Sox someday. I don't know if I will get into a game, but I take batting practice quite often. I'm not afraid. My eyes are still great, thank God. I sometimes think I am dreaming and I don't want to wake up. I want to stay in baseball the rest of my life."

I was grateful for the support of the fans, not only in Chicago, but throughout the big leagues. Columnist Joe Gergen described my first visit to Yankee Stadium in 1976. He observed how youngsters who were not even born when I made my last appearance in 1964 "had elbowed for position alongside the White Sox dugout, shoving their programs in the direction of the reborn man in navy blue uniform Number 9." He quoted a father as saying to his son: "Get Minnie Minoso before you get Martin," while the boy was eyeing the Yankee manager who was signing autographs nearby. "He was a helluva player," the father continued. His son, uncertain of his priorities, did what he was told.

I told newspapermen who were in the dugout with me: "To be in the big leagues again, to be part of this is something beautiful, the start of a new life. This is the fourth time I am back with the White Sox in some capacity. Chicago is my hometown and I am happy. The people, they were my universe. Thirty-five years I've been in baseball. What more can I ask than this? I have a new job, a job I love. I'm where everybody wants to be, in the big leagues."

After the enthusiasm of the first few weeks had worn off, I got down to the routine job of being a coach...hitting fungoes, throwing batting practice and generally helping the players as much as possible. I also *took* batting practice, to keep my eyes sharp and my swing level, causing much speculation as to whether Veeck would soon activate me as a player.

Well, the summer wore on and the Sox gradually slipped from contention. Still I kept taking batting practice. Along came September and to few people's surprise, I was activated. To some it may have appeared as a promotional gimmick by the master himself, Bill Veeck. However, Veeck seldom does anything without a reason, one that would help his ball club. I was delighted—my fourth decade as an active player, and I can't tell you how I looked forward to once again competing on the major league level.

No one, including Richards, was sure precisely how I would be used. I wasn't sure myself how I would react to major league pitching, although the prospect of facing it surely didn't frighten me. The date of my return to active duty was set as September 10. I was to be used at the discretion of the manager and I knew Richards would choose his spot well.

In his *Sun-Times* column, Joe Goddard wrote: "Now fifty-three years young and vigorous in body and spirit, Saturnino Orestes Arrieta Armas (Minnie) Minoso will be placed on the White Sox active roster Friday (the 10th) in time for a weekend series with the California Angels at Comiskey Park. He probably will be used by manager Paul Richards as a designated or pinch hitter, but just when is problematical. The Angels are pitching hard-throwing Nolan Ryan Friday night, to be followed by one of baseball's best lefties, Frank Tanana, Saturday. If Minoso had his druthers, he'd face the best. But against Ryan, Minoso not only would be at a righty-righty disadvantage, but probably would be overpowered. He is twenty-four years Ryan's senior. When Minnie officially bats, he will become the third oldest player in the history of the major leagues. Satchel Paige performed at age fifty-nine, and Nick Altrock at fifty-seven. Both were pitchers. He also will join Ted Williams,

Early Wynn and Mickey Vernon as the only players to perform in four decades."

Would I *ever* stop playing baseball? Probably not. I told the press: "I'll play 'til I'm dead, then I go up to heaven, see Babe Ruth and Lou Gehrig and my old friend Nellie Fox. We'll get up a game."

There were some complaints from a few players the week before about my taking batting practice. To that, Veeck remarked, "They probably saw Minnie put some balls into the upper deck while their's were only going out to the warning track." To which Richards added, "They (the players) ought to bow down at Minnie's feet. There's not a man on this team who could do what Minnie did."

My day of return, Friday, September 10, finally arrived. I was gratified to once again be an active player on the White Sox roster, a quarter of a century after my rookie year. It was another dream come true, one of the most cherished in my life. "See, I can still do it," I told teammates and reporters as I lined a ball into the stands during batting practice. In fact, I took a full thirty minutes of batting practice prior to our opening game with the Angels. Although I was eligible, Richards decided to hold me until Saturday in order for me to have the righty-lefty advantage against Frank Tanana.

All the while, Veeck denied my activation was a gimmick, a way to get people to the ballpark. Said he in response to this charge: "It's not quite fair to put it that way. I'm curious myself. I want to see if he can still hit. And frankly, I think he can."

Saturday would be the day, the day I would step to the plate in Comiskey Park for the first time in twelve years. Richards placed me ninth in the batting order as the designated hitter. My first time at bat in my fourth decade came with one out in the third. Kevin Bell was on third after hitting a triple to right center. It was music (with a Latin rhythm) to my ears as I heard field announcer Bob Finnegan intone: "Number 9, Minnie Minoso." Immediately before that moment, as I left the dugout for the on-deck circle, one of my teammates remarked somewhat disparagingly of my changes against the pitcher, Frank

Tanana. I quickly replied, "Did you ever face Bob Feller?" I don't know if he was even born when I faced Feller for the first time.

It was a nostalgic and proud moment for me as I stepped to the plate. My thoughts went back to the 1950s when I played before the cheering fans at Comiskey Park. And I thought of my friends who were part of the old "Go, Go Sox," players whose exploits now live in record books and in the hearts of those fans who saw them play. I resolved to dedicate my first time at bat to my former teammate and good friend, Nellie Fox, a warm and decent man who died much too young.

Holtzman describes what happened next: "Minoso assumed his usual closed stance and went into a semi-crouch, hanging over the plate as he did in the '50s and '60s when he was seven times chosen on the American League's All-Star Team. But Tanana struck him out on three pitches. The first was a fastball and Minoso couldn't get the bat all the way around and grounded it foul, off to the right. He swung and missed at the next two pitches, both breaking balls."

I only hoped Nellie would understand.

Again, in the fifth inning, I came to bat with Bell, who had doubled, on second base. Still, success eluded me. I jumped at Tanana's first pitch and popped up to Jerry Remy at second. The crowd nonetheless applauded me. Oh, how I wanted a hit. Catcher Jim Essian patted me on the back when I reached the dugout steps as a sign of reassurance...I wanted that hit even more.

Holtzman continues to describe my less than illustrious Bicentennial debut: "Minoso's final time at bat came in the seventh. This time he took Tanana's first pitch for a called ball. He then flied out to right fielder Dan Briggs...Minoso could have had one more time at bat in the ninth, but manager Paul Richards withdrew him for a pinch hitter because Tanana had been replaced by right-hander Dick Drago."

I conceded my timing was off. "I felt funny the first time," I told reporter. "I was so anxious to do everything correctly, and especially for my friend Nellie Fox. Then my timing improved

in my second and third at-bats..." After the game, I remained
for television interviews and stayed for another twenty minutes
signing autographs for youngsters. Responding to one fan who
commented on my lack of success, I said, "That's what makes
baseball great. You never know what's going to happen. You
know what also makes baseball great? You people—you're the
ones who make it great."

Holtzman ended his report by writing: "Some fans may believe that reactivating Minoso was nothing more than a cheap
publicity stunt. But...Minoso's sincerity and his enthusiasm
made it an occasion to remember. He'll be in the lineup again
Sunday when the Sox meet the Angels in the first game of a
double-header."

My comeback was a hitless one, but at age fifty-three, it was
great, if not miraculous to be back. In fact, I suppose I could
have been called the "hitless wonder" that afternoon, bringing
to mind the 1906 White Sox, a notoriously weak-hitting team,
who beat the powerpacked Cubs in the city's only crosstown
World Series, one which both northsiders and southsiders will
never forget—albeit for different reasons. Well, hitless or not,
Bill Veeck had said years before: "Ponce de Leon was wrong in
trying to find the Fountain of Youth in Florida. He should have
looked in Cuba. Minnie himself is *The* Fountain of Youth."

Tanana was a good pitcher and I felt his pitches were compa-
rable to those I looked at in my prime. Neither my eyes nor my
age were to blame for my 0 for 3. I place the blame squarely on
my lack of continuity in the majors. I believe in all honesty that
had I remained active in the big leagues instead of playing in
Mexico, I might have still been a strong and useful player. Even
at age fifty-three, some people were concerned about my age,
but all I can say is that individuals differ in their aging. My performance and durability in the Triple A Mexican Leagues
should have been taken into consideration. I had competed
among tough, young players—with a considerable degree of
success.

Now, though, my hero and inspiration was Satchel Paige.
Old Satch is gone now, but he seemed to be a master of durabil-

ity and perpetual rejuvenation. He was an outstanding player in his late fifties. Oftentimes, management imposes retirement upon men who are still strong, because they feel a man cannot perform past a certain age. America places too much emphasis on the so-called "youth cult," and most people accept this without argument. If a baseball player can perform to the utmost, his age should not be a decisive factor. Take Boston's Carl Yastrzemski, for example, still going strong in his forties. And Pete Rose, and Jim Kaat, and Gaylord Perry.... A man should be allowed to demonstrate his capabilities until he, himself, realizes the time has come to resign. When that time arises, at whatever age, the elders have the responsibility to step aside and make room for new blood.

One of the greatest milestones in my career occurred the following day. We played the Angels in a double-header and my name was entered in the first game's lineup as the designated hitter. In my first at-bat, I lined a fast ball off left-hander Sid Monge to left field for a base hit. With that liner, I became the oldest player in major league history to get a base hit. For me, it was 1951 all over again. I was nervous the previous day and I admit to overstriding. I felt less anxious on Sunday and was able to loosen up a bit.

For a moment, the crowd seemed awed that the old man actually managed to get a hit. Then I heard the words that had echoed in my ears and in my dreams for thirteen years...the crowd began the rhythmic chant, "Go, go, go—" It was one of the most beautiful sounds I ever heard. Second base was occupied, much to my relief, and I couldn't "go."

When I was stranded on the basepaths after the inning ended and began trotting back to the dugout, Angels third baseman Bill Melton congratulated me and umpire Dave Phillips applauded. I was humbled by these gestures of goodwill. It was Melton, remember, who, when he was starring for the White Sox passed me as the team's all-time home run leader. I had 135; Melton, 154. To end my second day's activity, I went down swinging and flied out. I played in one other game that year and my Bicentennial statistics read eight at bats, one hit and a batting average of .125.

Before spring training began for the 1977 season, Roland Hemond assigned me to spend three days in Puerto Rico conducting a baseball clinic organized by Puerto Rican sportswriter Luis Rodriguez Mayoral. During my visit, I met some old friends and renewed acquaintances with such former stars as Vic Power, Ruben Gomez, Sungo Carrera and others. I feasted on agasajos, played dominoes with Puerto Rican champions and toured the magnificent island.

The people of Puerto Rico were enthusiastic about my comeback and showed their feelings in a number of ways. For example, I received a trophy bearing the six flags of the Latin American countries represented in the Caribbean Federation of Baseball. Industrialization and modernization had firmly planted themselves in Puerto Rican soil. One thing, however, remained unchanged: the eternal love and warmth of its people who are always ready to open their arms and their homes to visitors.

Working with the teenagers at the baseball clinics was a rare pleasure. These youngsters, I am confident, profited immensely from these clinics, learning from the professionals involved. Proof can be seen in the great number of stars who continually emerge from Puerto Rico, many of whom participated in these clinics.

The year 1977 witnessed a change in management at the White Sox. My friend Paul Richards had, in the final days of the 1976 campaign, expressed to me that he was feeling tired. "Minnie," he said one day, "if I gave you the team, would you like to have it?" I told him that his coaching staff thought he'd last ten more years in the game. I didn't answer his question, but assured him his coaches would help in any way possible; all he would have to do is give the orders and we'd do the job in the field.

The change, nonetheless, came about. News reached me by way of a phone call. "Hi, Minnie!" said the voice on the other end of the line. "Do you know who's speaking to you? I'm the guy who kept you in the league for such a long time. I hope you can keep working for me." The voice belonged to one of the greatest pitchers of recent times: Bob Lemon. He had just been named manager of the Sox, replacing Richards. I responded. "OK, boss, I'll do whatever you say." We talked for a while, reminiscing of the "good old days" and making plans for next year's spring training in Sarasota.

When Lemon mentioned that he kept me in the league, he must have remembered the mid-1950s when, on occasion, I hit him quite well. In July of 1954, for example, I had four homers against Cleveland; three at Bob's expense. I also broke up his no-hitter on opening day in 1954. The following year, Lemon beat us 5-1 in the opener and I batted in the run to spoil the shut-out. No wonder so many people called us "cousins."

I once again signed on as first-base coach and Larry Doby came in as batting instructor. That spring some eighty players competed to make the team—minor leaguers, rookies, free agents.... Our final roster comprised what we thought was a winning team and included two outstanding power hitters: Richie Zisk and Oscar Gamble. These two didn't disappoint us and hit seventy homeruns between them in 1977. Still, we had to be content with a third place finish and a record of 90-72. The pitching was in need of improvement, but the Sox were doubtlessly coming alive once again, and the fans were beginning to revive the old excitement and spirit that was so much a part of the Go-Gox Sox of the '50s.

I worked hard as a coach that season, in addition to making numerous speaking engagements on behalf of the organization. During that year, I learned a great deal from Lemon. He was like Paul Richards in a number of ways, a man who always remained composed even if a catastrophe befell him. During his pitching days, Lemon was something of an extrovert, but his personality turned inward when he began to manage.

Bob lasted until the middle of the 1978 season when rumors were confirmed and he was replaced by Larry Doby. I had coached at first during those early months of the 1978 season, but rumors also had me making a change to concentrate more on public relations and community work. Upon return from a road trip, Roland Hemond called to say Bill Veeck wanted to meet with me. I was anxious, because I knew of the rumors that were circulating.

Bill didn't beat around the bush. He told me straight out that I was to devote my time to public relations and communications work for the White Sox. He felt it would benefit the entire organization and that, besides, I had already fulfilled the necessary time to qualify for my pension in the majors. Bill insisted I work with the players during pre-game practice, wearing my Number 9 so the fans could see I was there. Part of my new duties also included walking through the stands during home games, making myself visible and meeting with the fans. Veeck said if I was not in agreement, I should tell him frankly and he would reassign me as coach the following year. I told Papa Veeck that since he was the person who had brought me into baseball I knew he would never harm my career. Veeck added he knew it would be difficult at first because of my love for the game. "But let's give it a try," he concluded.

At first, it was indeed difficult for me to work away from the playing field. Most of my life was spent outdoors, either playing ball or harvesting sugar cane. I missed being in the first base coaches' box, being in direct contact with the fans and living each play of the game. Some fans even expressed the opinion that it was not the same without me. But as time wore on, I became more used to my role and looked forward with increasing eagerness to each new day on the Sox public relations team.

Replacing me as first base coach was Tony La Russa. Doby finished the 1978 season and was in turn replaced by Don Kessinger, the former great shortstop of the Cubs. Gradually, my active participation on the field waned and ended with spring training in 1980. Few would have imagined that I was not through swinging a bat in the majors.

None of the stars of Saturday's 4-2 White Sox victory over California had even been born when Minnie Minoso played in his first major league game. Saturday, they shared a moment in the spotlight with the fifty-seven-year-old wonder, who became the second player in history to appear in a major-league game in each of five decades. Minoso appeared as a pinch batter to start the Sox seventh, and, after taking two low sliders from Angel pitcher Frank Tanana, lofted a high foul to catcher Dave Skages. "It was just a little bit on the outside corner," said Minnie, who may have lost the timing, but not the eye that made him a lifetime .298 hitter over 10 seasons.

—*Robert Markus, Chicago Tribune, October 5, 1980.*

Minnie Minoso, reactivated at the age of fifty-seven, Saturday became the second major league player to play in five different decades, and after the game said, "I think I can play until I die." Minoso's appeared as a seventh-inning pinch batter for Greg Pryor. Frank Tanana, the Angel's starter, tipped his cap in salute, as Minoso swung two bats in the on-deck circle . . . Minoso, who will appear again in Sunday's regular season finale, expressed disappointment with his inability to get a hit off Tanana. "I had a lot of confidence and saw the ball all right," he said. Minoso also said that, if possible, he would like to play in "ten decades."

—*Jerome Holtzman, Chicago Sun-Times, October 5, 1980.*

Saturnino Orestes Arrieta Armas Minoso—one name for each of the five decades in which the venerable "Minnie" will have appeared in the major leagues. Minoso is being activated for the final three Chicago White Sox games this weekend, and who said departing owner Bill Veeck didn't have one last trick up his sleeve? At fifty-seven, Minoso—assuming he gets in there one time against California—would be the oldest known big-league baseball player this side of Satchel Paige. The only other to pull the five-decade stunt was Nick Altrock, the Washington Senator pitcher and coach better known as a diamond clown.

—*Byron Rose, Washington Post, October 2, 1980.*

Top of the 9th

The year 1980 saw the realization of one of my most significant records as a major leaguer. Once again I demonstrated my durability. The Sox reactivated me as a player for their last series in September. Thus, at age fifty-seven, I was going to play in my fifth decade as a major leaguer. It was a milestone that was recorded on sports pages throughout the country and even overseas. Only Nick Altrock could claim that feat, having pitched with the old Louisville National League ballclub beginning in 1898 and in succeeding decades with the White Sox and Washington.

Regarding my comeback, Byron Rosen of the Washington Post commented: "Saturnino Orestes Arrieta Armas Minoso, one name for each of the five decades in which the venerable Minnie will have appeared in the major leagues."

That was the year Oakland's Rickie Henderson broke Ty Cobb's 65-year-old American League record with his 97th stolen base. Rose continued: "Minoso averaged 26 a year in winning successive AL theft titles in 1951-52-53. But in that era, the young Cuban was a real flash. The league's 1950 leader was Dom DiMaggio, 15 steals."

My return sparked the usual queries of comparisons of players today versus those during the '50s when I broke into the majors. I could only answer that there is great talent today but, as I told Dennis Lustig of the *Cleveland Plain Dealer,* "don't take anything away from the old talent. How many fastballers are there today like Bob Feller? Who can throw a curve like Camilo Pascual? Who has a pitching staff like Wynn, Lemon and Score? With all my respect for everyone, a Ted Williams comes along once every 50 years. There is only one Ted. Only one Stan."

Lustig said I was on Cloud Nine because I was back in baseball. To which I replied, "I sometimes think I am dreaming and I don't want to wake up... I want to stay in baseball the rest of my life."

My day came on October 5, 1980, and as luck would have it we were again playing the Angels and the opposing pitcher was Frank Tanana, the exact same match-up as four years earlier when I played in my fourth decade of big league ball. I pinched hit in the seventh inning for Greg Pryor and, as I took my practice swings in the on-deck circle, Tanana stood on the mound and tipped his hat in salute to me.

His first two pitches were balls, but his third was a sinker around my knees and I took a cut at it. Unfortunately, I swung too late and popped up in foul territory to the right of the plate. I was confident and I saw the ball all right. I was pleased Tanana didn't float a lollipop to the plate so I could get a hit. He pitched me the same as he did anybody else.

Tony La Russa was by then the manager, and he told the press: "It was a privilege for me to tell him to grab a bat. Minnie commands everybody's respect and it was a personal honor for me to write his name into the lineup card and tell the umpire he was hitting."

La Russa admits to first-hand experience about the special rapport between the fans and me. Remember, it was Tony who replaced me as first-base coach in 1978. As he tells it, "I wasn't too popular with the fans for awhile."

I still had one more at-bat, though. Tony sent me to the plate in the season's finale, but again I failed by popping up to the catcher.

So much for my *fifth* decade. I wonder if Tanana and I can get together again in 1990 for decade number six?

The man (Minoso) still can play baseball. In an old-timers game in Miami a few weeks ago, there was a $100 prize for the first one to hit a single. Minoso won it. There was $100 for the first to hit a double. Minoso won that, too. "I'll always be able to play. I take care of myself," he said.

—*Joe Goddard, Chicago Sun-Times, 1982.*

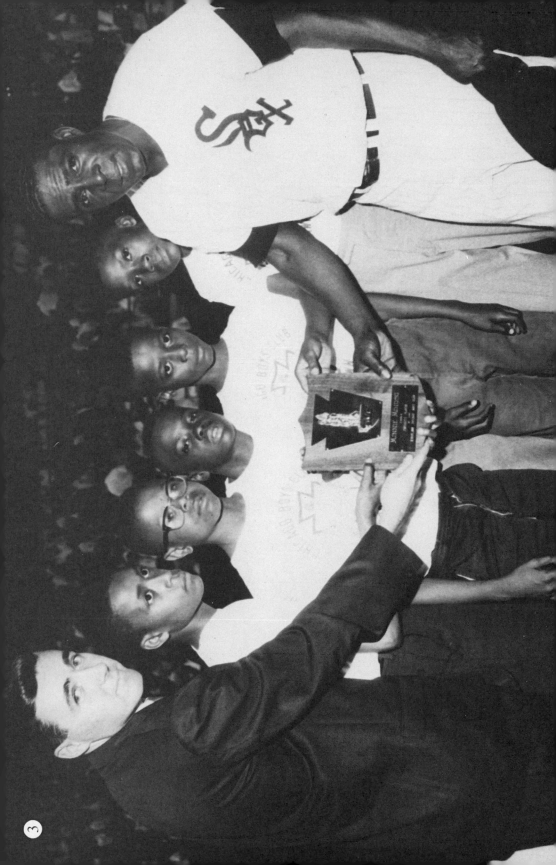

③

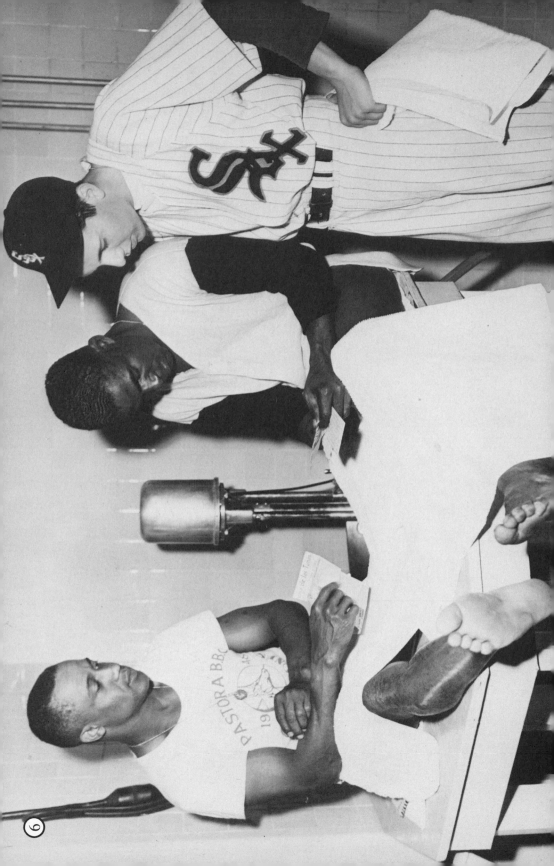

MINOSO 9

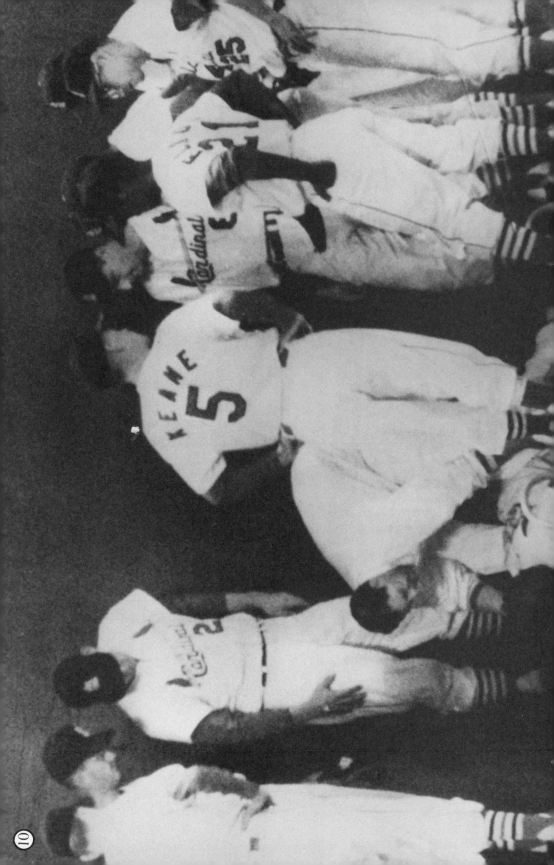

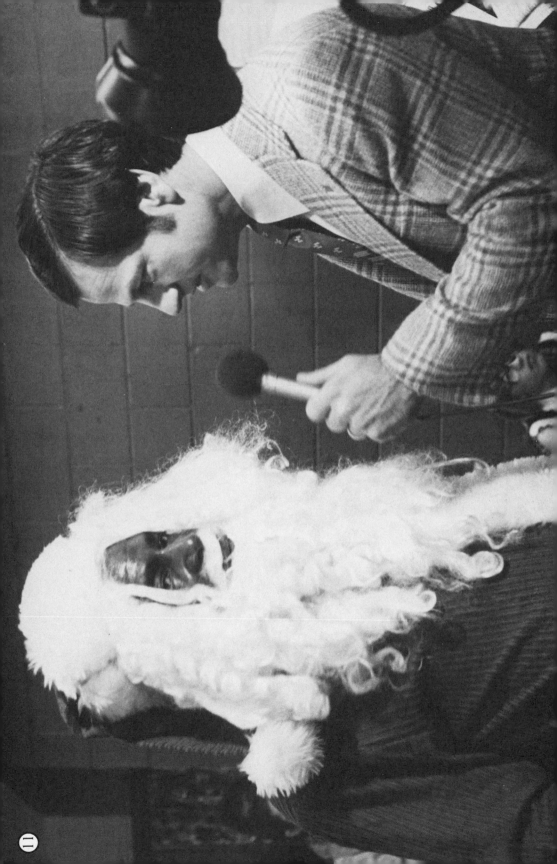

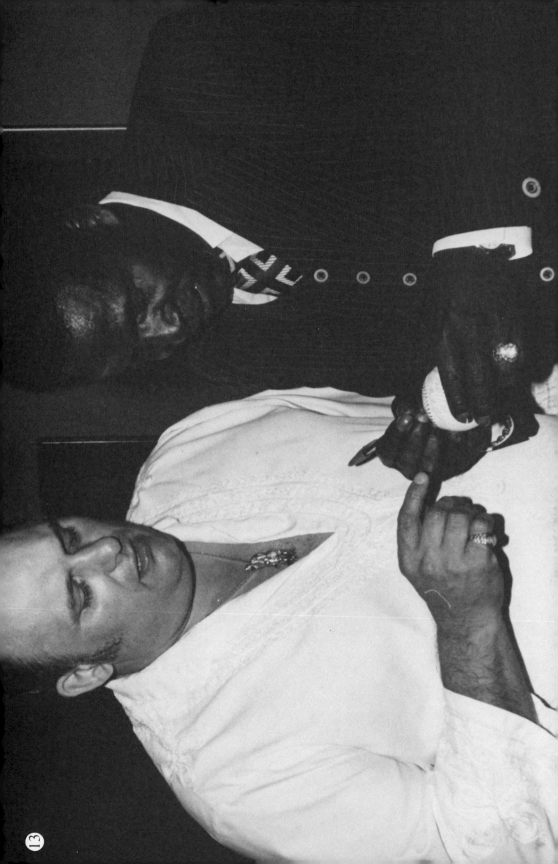

(1) Minnie's career, depicted in this section shows, particularly in the caricature on the first page, that his popularity has never waned. (2) On the second page Minnie and teammates Landis, Aparicio, and Fox receive the Rawlings Gold Glove Award. (3) Always popular with youngsters, the next page illustrates this as Minnie receives an award from members of the Chicago Boys Club. (4) Next, Minnie crosses the plate after his first home run in a Sox uniform.

Photo number (5) illustrates only one of the many times Minnie was hit by pitches. This one was in Yankee Stadium in 1955. (6) A whirlpool bath was always on Minnie's schedule. (7) Next, Minnie hits a game-winning home run April 19, 1960 against Kansas City. (8) Minnie dons the new White Sox uniform.

In photo number (9), Minnie steals second and goes on to score the winning run in a game against the Washington Senators, April 24, 1961. (10) Minnie collides with the left field wall in Busch Stadium May 12, 1962 sustaining a skull fracture that kept him out of action for several months. (11) Then, telecaster Johnny Morris interviews a disguised Minnie at one of his frequent community appearances. (12) (13) (14) Always a favorite of fans of all ages, Minnie obliges with autographs whenever and wherever asked. (15) Minnie's last at bat against Frank Tanana on October 5, 1980.

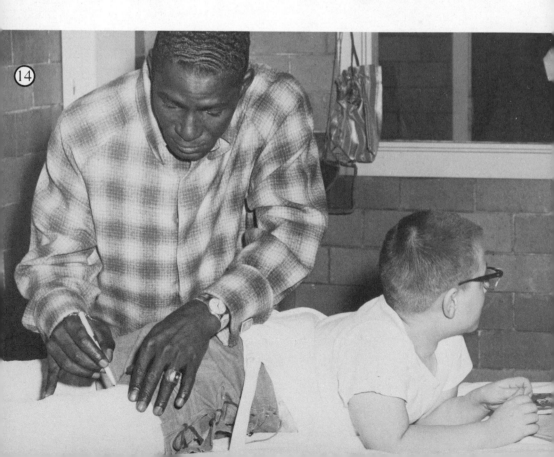

Bottom of the 9th

I concentrate my efforts now on public relations work for the White Sox and special duties for another employer, C & K Distributors. Company President Jerry Campagna is a popular Chicago-area businessman and is married to a compatriot of mine, Juanita, a beautiful lady who was born and raised not far from my El Perico home.

My association with C & K Distributors began in the latter part of 1976 when a friend of mine, Tony Perez, who worked in C & K's public relations department suggested I meet with Campagna. He invited me to a softball game for a league Mr. Campagna was sponsoring. After the game, they asked me to dinner for the team's players where Jerry inquired if I would agree to attend a luncheon soon to discuss business. I agreed. A few days later, Jerry, his company's secretary/treasurer Bill Hansa and I met in a Rush Street restaurant where they inquired if I would be willing to work for C & K-Old Style in the public relations/community department. I told them'd I'd be delighted. A short time later, I reported to the company's southside headquarters. There I was introduced to Lulo Felipez, vice-president in charge of the Hispanic Market in Chicago and John Shea, the advertising and public relations director. These two gentlemen would provide my weekly and daily assignments.

In addition to speaking engagements, I do special promotion for the beer distributed by C & K, the largest Heileman wholesale distributor in the world. Although other distributors have tried to entice me away from C & K, I declined, because Campagna, like my Papa Veeck, helped me at a difficult time in my life in reinstating me in Chicago. I owe them my loyalty. I could never express totally my appreciation to the Sox and C & K for helping to make my return to my "rebirth" in Chicago so successful.

In my capacity as a special coach with the Sox, I practice with the team before each home game. At times, I also take a few cuts with the bat, *just in case* the Sox might want to reactive me again someday. While I'm on the field, I respond to the fans who gather as close to the field as they can get by signing autographs, programs, gloves, baseballs and whatever else they may have and to answer their questions. I've always had that special place in my heart for the children and I often give away baseballs I have purchased and Sox' broken bats that I have mended with nails and tapes to serve as personal souvenirs of their favorite big league team.

When performing my duties for the White Sox or C & K, a typical day could go something like this: Pauline Allyn, Director of Community Relations for the Sox, or Lulo Felipez of C & K, may assign me to make a presentation or attend a special gathering. It may be nearby or a hundred miles away. I've even travelled to different states and foreign countries. I've thus made presentations in a wide range of places and settings, from a jail to an orphanage and have mingled with a variety of people. After all, people have always been my business.

I have become adept at improvising my speeches and presentations according to the audience. I'm always alert to the moods and needs of the moment. Baseball is, naturally, the basic subject matter, but to young people, I always emphasize the principles of good citizenship, schooling and respect. I always remark how vitally important it was for me, as a major leaguer, to display a certain demeanor, and how I believe all major league players should do so.

Experience has taught me there are many ingredients, even seemingly insignificant ones, that contribute to the manner in which popular sports figures are "idolized" by many fans, especially children. It would be a terrible mistake to spoil this charm, this mysterious fascination which has developed between the hero and his admirers. When the fans cheer for individual players, they don't consider nationality, race or color, but simply the athlete himself. That is why this player has the obligation to be a sportsman on and off the field. Any player who lets pride and vanity replace personal friendliness and respectability is asking for a tremendous emotional letdown, for his name may appear in the headlines one day and seemingly the next, when his playing days are behind him, he is again simply another citizen.

I tried at all times to be just Orestes Minoso, the cane-cutter who had known poverty and who was fortunate to possess the talents which allowed him to rise above this poverty. But whenever I returned to Cuba, I used to go to the same places as always, among the poor people, where I could play dominoes and take part in their activities.

I wanted my actions at all times to be spontaneous and natural, and lacking in hypocrisy. For example, if I were on the highway and noticed a car in trouble, I would stop and help. Often, I came to the aid of the aged. I did this not as a publicity stunt or to increase my popularity, but merely out of concern. I could never forget my humble beginnings and I was still the same Minoso. These acts were my way of thanking the Lord for what he had granted me. I always felt we were all under God's scrutiny and I tried to live my life accordingly. I have always thanked Him for giving me the strength and talents I needed to succeed.

Even my license plate spells "Minoso." Obviously, this sometimes hinders my getting to places on time because I'm often hailed down for an impromptu autograph session. That's okay with me, especially when the kids are yelling "Minnie, Minnie" as I drive past. I even carry some souvenir caps in my car and stop whenever I can to autograph and give them to kids. It's heartwarming when a youngster comes up to me and says that his dad remembers seeing me play and he says you were one of the best.

Well if his "Dad" says I was one of the best...!

The questions asked me at the gatherings I attend usually follow a set pattern: how have I preserved my health and endurance; do I have managerial ambitions; do I still play or manage outside the U.S.; how many autographs have I signed and does this cause an inconvenience, etc. etc.? The kids are always curious about my records. They want advice on how to play the game better and ask many technical questions about baseball. I'm more than happy to answer these questions and, especially, to provide pointers on how youngsters should approach the game. To potential pitchers, I tell them to perfect the fastball before learning other sophisticated pitches so their throwing arm does not tire. If I find a youngster with superior abilities I prompt him to one day try out for the Sox. I tell them that, though "diamonds-in-the-rough" may be found occasionally on the sandlots, good players are generally found by big league scouts in the little leagues and in high school and college leagues. Generally, scouts travel to organized settings to "discover" promising young players. Seldom, I might add, do they miss a promising young man. Also, I assure these youngsters, that discrimination does not exist nowadays. The emphasis is on quality and ability. Most important, baseball should be in their blood and in their mind, not just in physical attributes.

Baseball has, indeed, been in my blood and in my mind, from the sugar cane fields of Cuba to the big leagues, into Mexico and back to the White Sox. As the old sayings go, a baseball game is never over until the last man is out, and baseball is a nine inning game. Well, I'm not out yet, and what's more, I'll be in the lineup *after* the ninth inning.

"Minnie doesn't seem to have any regrets. He accepts life for what it has provided. Too many people, I think, feel sorry for themselves for things they seem to think they deserve, but have been denied. Minnie, though, is grateful for the good things that have happened... All too often, big name guest speakers arrive late and leave as soon as the program is over. Not Minnie! He stays around to answer questions and to sign autographs, no matter how long it takes. The size of the line—usually kids—doesn't matter. No one who wants his autograph goes away empty-handed."

—Roland A. Hemond,
Executive Vice President/General Manager,
Chicago White Sox, 1982.

Extra-Innings

Chicago is my home now and I hope I'll never again have to make another "comeback." I've had offers to manage outside the United States, but I prefer to remain here. I make no secret of the fact that I would welcome an opportunity to manage in the majors or Triple A, but short of this I still enjoy my work with the Sox and C & K and find it personally rewarding to meet with people who share the same love for baseball as I have.

I find working with youth the most fulfilling of all. During the spring and summer months I often devote time to the Little Leagues. The youngsters may one day aspire to being professional baseball players; perhaps not. But what they will all be are citizens and I hope that, in working with them, I can, by instruction and by example, teach them to give their best at all times, to never quit no matter how discouraging the situation may be.

Baseball, and all team sports for that matter, teaches one to pull together with others for the good of all. It instills discipline and the acceptance of responsibility. It also helps one to accept defeat gracefully. Baseball must be put into perspective. To these kids it is an important part of their lives; and they're right, though not necessarily in the final score—whether their team wins or loses. It is, rather, a time which will impress a lasting effect on their lives regardless of the paths they choose for their careers.

Helping these youngsters is an uplifting experience. Their exuberance, their enthusiasm to just "play ball" keeps me thinking young.

I enjoy being the good will ambassador for the White Sox. I hope that I'll always be able to pull on my Old Number 9 and go out onto the field during batting practice at Comiskey Park. Posing for photos with the fans, signing autographs and meeting with the people are things I delight in doing. And I truly hope my presence will remain in demand and that I'll always be welcome as a guest speaker whether as a representative of the White Sox or C & K.

Often, I encounter discussions which I'm sure most former big leaguers have been involved in. Comparisons and dreams of what might have been are hot stove league banterings that are inevitable. How, for example, would I have fared today if I were playing in my prime?

Roland Hemond assures us, "He'd be in the Top Ten in hitting. And he'd be among the highest paid."

That's good news, but unfortunately impossible to prove. I'd like to think I could be right up there in hitting with such current stars as Rod Carew, George Brett, Robin Yount, Eddie Murray and other American League batting leaders.

And what about the Hall of Fame?

Hemond admits I would have been seriously considered had I entered the majors at an earlier age. He and others seem to think that becoming a major leaguer at age twenty-even, two years after Jackie Robinson broke the "color barrier" hurt my chances. "If Minoso had begun his major league career at age twenty-one or twenty-two," observes Hemond, "he would have, I am quite sure, accumulated an impressive array of statistics for consideration for enshrinement in the Hall."

Perhaps I would have been considered, perhaps not. What matters, though, is that I have years of baseball memories to look back on, years of accomplishment in which I not only put my name into the record books, but also made lasting friendships. But as Old Satch used to say, "Don't look back, 'cause someone may be gaining on you." For me, the future is bright indeed. I intend to keep actively associated with professional baseball, and especially with the White Sox, just as long as I am able to contribute—to their popularity in meeting with the fans and to the Club, by helping the young players develop their potential. And if I ever do leave baseball, I want to go out with my head high.

As must be obvious to everyone, my autobiography is far from complete. Tomorrow and the next day and years to come will add still more innings to the scoreboard of this former cane-cutter from sunny Cuba. But my autobiography would not be complete without an expression of gratitude to all those who have made my baseball dreams come true, to make it possible for me to be able to reminisce in these pages about my fulfilling life. I came from humble beginnings and to hear the fans cheering me on as a big leaguer was more than I could have hoped for in those days I ran with abandon as a boy in the fields of the sugar mills. I'm proud that I have nothing to hide and that my only obsession was to perfect my abilities on the baseball diamond and my capacity to help others.

Tragedy, heartbreak and personal loss are part of everyone's life. No less mine. I always keep in touch with my children and with my former wife who now lives in another city. Orestes, Jr., as I said, is working for the Jehovah's Witness Church and residing in the Chicago area. My father died in 1977 at his retirement home in the province of Camaguey. Due to travel complications between the United States and Cuba, I could not attend his funeral and had to resign myself to praying that he and my beloved mother were once again together. My brother Francisco, who grew up with me and was himself considered a baseball prospect, passed away in 1981, also in Cuba. My sisters, Juana and Flora Maria, together with my younger brother Carlitos Arrieta, are still residing in Cuba and in their home they keep for me many of the trophies I found necessary to leave behind.

And lastly, I thank God for granting me the potential to play baseball. I made a living out of doing what I truly loved, and in the process, developed bonds of friendship and rapport with fans which shall never diminish.

I am proud of my personal records in baseball, a career

which, of course, is not over because I'm still very much a part of the game. But I do not know what destiny has in store for me, but I will accept whatever it may be. If I'm given new assignments, I guarantee I'll perform them with the same intensity, the same dedication and the same energy and interest which characterized my way of playing baseball during my five decades in professional baseball.

Regardless, though, of what I'm doing or where destiny may take me, my heart and memories will return to the game and the fans I love. And the shouts of "Go-Minnie-Go," and "Go-Sox-Go" will echo through my soul and I will be filled with pride and happiness.

In closing, may I say to you, "No digo adios, sino hasta luego," which is Spanish for, *this is not goodbye; instead only so long for awhile.* In other words, I'll be around.

THE CUBAN RECORD
(Professional and Winter League)
ORESTES MINOSO
(The Cuban Meteorite)

Year	Club	G	AB	R	H	TB	2b	3b	HR	RBI	SB	BA
1945-46	Marianao	37	143	14	42	53	7	2	0	13	5	.294(*)
1946-47	Marianao	64	253	36	63	82	9	5	0	20	7	.249
1947-48	Marianao	70	270	43	77	121	15	13**	1	36	7	.285
1948-49	Marianao	69	260	42	69	99	8	5	4	27	9	.263
1949-50	Did Not Play											
1950-51	Marianao	66	252	54	81	117	12	6	4	41	10	.321
1951-52	Marianao	42	144	19	39	53	6	1	2	10	1	.271
1952-53	Marianao	71	266	67(:*)	87	145(::)	9	5	13	42	13	.327
1953-54	Marianao	47	176	25	52	94	9	3	9	36	2	.295
1954-55	Did Not Play											
1955-56	Marianao	64	252	47	69	109	10	3	8	35	8	.274
1956-57	Marianao	50	218	40	68	108	13	3	7	38	0	.312
1957-58	Marianao	58	238	37	60	94	9	1	8	34	3	.252
1958-59	Marianao	55	223	33	60	85	8	1	5	25	6	.269
1959-60	Marianao	45	169	25	39	58	3	2	4	23	4	.231
1960-61	Marianao	35	128	12	32	44	7	1	1	12	1	.250

(*) Declared Rookie of the Year.

In 13 years of participation in Cuban baseball, Minoso batted 2,992 times and had 838 hits for an average of .280. He had a total of 66 home runs

(**) More 3b hits in one year than any other player.

(:*) More runs scored in one season than any other player.

More home runs (5) in 4 consecutive games than any other player (November 9, 11, 14, 15, 1952).

(::) More total bases in one season than any other player.

Leader in being	1956-57	11	
hit by pitches	1957-58	15	(Record in Cuba)
	1958-59	10	
	1959-60	7	

THE CAREER
SATURNINO ORESTES ARRIETA MINOSO (ARMAS)
(Minnie)
Chicago White Sox

Born November 29, 1922, at Perico, Matanzas, Cuba.
Height, 5'11". Weight, 175.
Threw and batted righthanded.
Hobbies—Movies and horseback riding.

Led American League in stolen bases (31) 1951, (22) 1952, (25) 1953.
Established major league records for most consecutive years leading league hit by pitcher (6), 1956 through 1961; and most years leading league in hit by pitcher (10), 1961.
Established American League record for most times hit by pitch, career, 189, 1949 through 1964 (except 1950 and 1962).
Led American League in total bases with 304 in 1954.
Named by THE SPORTING NEWS as American League Rookie of the Year, 1951.
Named as outfielder on THE SPORTING NEWS All-Star Major League Teams 1959-60.
Received Gold Glove award as outstanding major league fielder in left field, 1957; received award as outstanding American League fielder in left field, 1959-60.

Year	Club	League	Pos.	G.	AB.	R.	H.	2B.	3B.	HR.	RBI.	B.A.	PO.	A.	E.	F.A.
1948—Dayton	Cent.	3B-2B	11	40	14	21	7	1	1	8	.525	6	26	0	1.000
1949—Cleveland	Amer.	OF	9	16	2	3	0	0	1	1	.188	11	0	0	1.000
1949—San Diego	P.C.	OF	137	532	99	158	19	7	22	75	.297	309	10	12	.964
1950—San Diego	P.C.	3B-O-SS	169	599	130	203	40	10	20	115	.339	209	290	*33	.938
1951—Cleve.†-Chi.	Am.	O-3-1-S	146	530	112	173	34	*14	10	76	.326	264	130	22	.947
1952—Chicago	Am.	OF-3B-SS	147	569	96	160	24	9	13	61	.281	323	22	7	.980
1953—Chicago	Am.	•OF-3B	151	556	104	174	24	8	15	104	.313	282	29	•12	.963
1954—Chicago	Am.	OF-3B	153	568	119	182	29	*13	19	116	.320	347	25	9	.976
1955—Chicago	Am.	OF-3B	139	517	79	149	26	7	10	70	.288	289	21	9	.972
1956—Chicago	Am.	OF-3B-1B	151	545	106	172	29	•11	21	88	.316	287	16	10	.968
1957—Chicago‡	Am.	OF-3B	153	568	96	176	•36	5	12	103	.310	293	9	5	.984
1958—Cleveland	Am.	OF-3B	149	556	94	168	25	2	24	80	.302	301	13	8	.975
1959—Cleveland§	Am.	OF	148	570	92	172	32	0	21	92	.302	314	14	5	.985
1960—Chicago	Am.	OF	*154	591	89	*184	32	4	20	105	.311	282	14	6	.980
1961—Chicago x	Am.	OF	152	540	91	151	28	3	14	82	.280	273	10	13	.956
1962—St. Louis yz	Nat.	OF	39	97	14	19	5	0	1	10	.196	33	2	1	.972
1963—Washington a	Am.	OF-3B	109	315	38	72	12	2	4	30	.229	108	26	5	.964
1964—Chicago b	Am.	OF	30	31	4	7	0	0	1	5	.226	9	0	0	1.000
1964—Indianapolis	P.C.	OF-3B	52	178	22	47	11	0	4	26	.264	50	36	9	.905
1965—Jalisco	Mex.	OF-3B	134	469	*106	169	*35	10	14	82	.360	478	19	11	.978
1966—Jalisco c	Mex.	1B	107	376	70	131	18	1	6	45	.348	922	48	*19	.981
1967—Orizaba d	Mex. SE	OF-3B-1B	36	100	20	35	7	3	5	19	.350	76	13	7	.927
1967—Jalisco	Mex.	1B-OF	13	37	5	9	1	2	0	3	.243	78	2	0	1.000

Year—Club	League	Pos.	G	AB	R	H	2B	3B	HR	RBI	B.A.	PO	A.	E.	F.A.
1968—Puerto Mexico d	Mex. SE	1B-OF-3B	56	145	30	53	17	2	4	23	.366	181	9	8	.960
1968—Jalisco	Mex.	OF-1B	22	54	9	16	5	1	2	13	.296	24	2	0	1.000
1969—Puerto Mexico d	Mex. SE	1B-OF	74	193	33	58	10	2	2	32	.301	448	2	9	.981
1969—Jalisco	Mex.	1B-OF-3B	36	103	18	33	3	1	2	14	.320	214	11	2	.991
1970—Gomez Palacio d	Mex.	1B	40	47	6	22	6	0	6	17	.468	25	1	1	.963
1971—Gomez Palacio d	Mex.	1B-2B	112	336	37	106	15	2	6	57	.315	807	29	11	.987
1972—Gomez Palacio	Mex.	1B	181	425	48	121	24	1	12	63	.285	1015	36	10	.991
1973—Gomez Palacio	Mex.	1B-OF	120	407	50	108	5	1	12	83	.265	852	25	10	.989
1976—Chicago	Amer.	PH/DH	3	8	0	1	0	0	0	0	.125	0	0	0	0
1980—Chicago	Amer.	PH	2	2	0	0	0	0	0	0	0	0	0	0	0
American League Totals			1791	6472	1122	1943	331	83	185	1013	.300	3383	329	111	.971
National League Totals			39	97	14	19	5	0	1	10	.196	33	2	1	.972
Major League Totals			1830	6589	1136	1962	336	83	186	1023	.299	3416	331	112	.971

† Traded to Chicago White Sox as part of three-club deal in which Indians also shipped Pitcher Sam Zoldak and Catcher Ray Murray to Philadelphia Athletics: Cleveland received Pitcher Lou Brissie from Athletics for their share of the players. Athletics also sent Outfielder Paul Lehner to the White Sox and added Outfielders Dave Philley and Gus Zernial from Sox, April 30, 1951.

‡ Traded to Cleveland Indians with Infielder Fred Hatfield for Pitcher Early Wynn and Outfielder Al Smith, December 4, 1957.

§ Traded to Chicago White Sox with Pitchers Don Ferrarese and Jake Striker and Catcher Dick Brown for Catcher John Romano, First Baseman Norm Cash and Third Baseman-Outfielder Bubba Phillips, December 5, 1959.

x Traded to St. Louis Cardinals for First Baseman-Outfielder Joe Cunningham, November 27, 1961.

y Suffered skull fracture and broken right wrist chasing line drive, May 11, 1962; returned to active list, July 19—used sparingly for remainder of season.

z Traded to Washington Senators for an estimated $30,000 and minor league player to be named later, April 2, 1963.

a Released, October 14, 1963; signed as free agent by Chicago White Sox, April 8, 1954.

b Released July 17, 1964.

c On disabled list, May 21 to June 30, 1966.

d Player-manager.

ALL-STAR GAME RECORD

Year	League	Pos.	AB	R	H	2B	3B	HR	RBI	B.A.	PO	A.	E.	F.A.
1951—American		OF	2	0	0	0	0	0	0	.000	2	0	0	1.000
1952—American		OF	1	1	1	0	0	0	1	1.000	0	0	0	.000
1953—American		OF	2	0	2	0	0	0	0	1.000	0	0	0	.000
1954—American		OF	4	1	2	1	0	0	1	.500	1	1	1	.500
1957—American		OF	1	0	1	0	0	0	1	1.000	0	1	0	1.000
1959—American (first game)		OF	5	0	0	0	0	0	0	.000	0	0	0	1.000
1960—American (both games)		OF	5	0	0	0	0	0	0	.000	1	0	0	1.000
All-Star Game Totals			20	2	6	2	0	0	2	.300	5	2	1	.875

RECORD AS MANAGER

Year	Club	League	W.	L.	Pos.
1967—Orizaba	Mex. SE		40	66	Seventh
1968—Puerto Mexico	Mex. SE		57	36	Third
1969—Puerto Mexico	Mex. SE		56	59	Fourth
1970—Gomez Palacio	Mex.		68	92	Third (N)
1971—Gomez Palacio	Mex.		72	76	Fourth (N)
1976—Leon	Mex. Cen.		28	39	Sixth

Coach Chicago White Sox, 1976